The Coming Crash
in the Housing Market

The Coming Crash in the Housing Market

10 Things You Can Do Now to Protect Your Most Valuable Investment

John R. Talbott

McGraw-Hill

New York Chicago San Francisco Lisbon
London Madrid Mexico City Milan New Delhi
San Juan Seoul Singapore Sydney Toronto

4 5 6 7 8 9 0   DOC/DOC   0 9 8 7 6 5 4 3

ISBN 0-07-142220-X

McGraw-Hill books are available at special discounts to use as premiums and sales promotions, or for use in corporate training programs. For more information, please write to the Director of Special Sales, Professional Publishing, McGraw-Hill, Two Penn Plaza, New York, NY 10121-2298. Or contact your local bookstore.

 This book is printed on recycled, acid-free paper containing a minimum of 50% recycled de-inked paper.

Library of Congress Cataloging-in-Publication Data

Talbott, John, 1955-
  The coming crash in the housing market : 10 things you can do now to protect your most valuable investment / by John Talbott.
       p. cm.
Includes bibliographical references.
  ISBN 0-07-142220-X (hardcover : alk. paper)
  1. Housing—Prices—United States. I. Title.
  HD7293.T36 2003
  333.33'82'0973—dc21
                                        2003002513

To my parents, my brothers and sisters,
my teachers, and my friends,
who instilled in me the desire to know why,
even regarding questions that already seemed answered

Contents

PART II

And What You Can Do About It

Preface

This book takes a different perspective than most books about real estate. First, it concerns itself with residential real estate, not office or commercial space. Much of the study of real estate concerns commercial real estate, as big corporations are the typical clients of most real estate advisory and consulting firms. Here the focus will be on the family home, specifically single-family houses and condominium apartments.

Second, most books that even address residential real estate look at it from the perspective of a real estate investor, someone who is looking to buy income-producing properties for investment potential. While this book will be very useful to such an investor, individual family homeowners and prospective homeowners—people just like you—are the primary audience. This book shows that it would be helpful for homeowners to start thinking more like investors, but we do not assume any special knowledge of finance or economics by readers in order to benefit from this book. While I make liberal use of charts in the book, the reader need not recognize any greater truth from them other than that a straight line up indicates a strong positive relationship.

It is really quite incredible that this book has not already been written. The average American homeowner has more equity capital invested in his or her home at current market prices than he or she does in his or her entire stock and bond portfolio. And yet when you tour the local bookstore, you will find thousands of books on portfolio investment strategy but very few, if any, that look at your home as a financial investment requiring active management. Sure, there are books on how to physically maintain and improve your property, a great growth opportunity for Home Depot and Lowe's. But how many books have you seen that attempt to explain what the value of your house is, what factors determine that value, what risks you face as a homeowner, and what you can do to preserve that value in an uncertain future?

Whenever market prices of anything trend upward for any significant period of time, there is a tendency in the popular media to talk about a bubble, the implication being not only that the market price is not stable but that it is in for an eventual popping. The problem with this type of analysis, of course, is that not all bubbles burst. Some growth trends that had all the makings of a bubble early on, continued to grow up to be very strong, stable companies. Ford Motor, after introducing the Model T, and Microsoft, more recently, come to mind.

In deciding whether the current housing market is due for a major correction, the challenge is determining whether the participants are acting irrationally or there is a systemic problem such that market forces cannot act to assure that overpricing does not occur. In fact here the supposed experts are quick to blame fallible humans for acting irrationally in overpaying for their homes. It is an easy argument to make and a difficult one to refute, in as much as we all know one or two irrational humans. However, this book argues that individual buyers and sellers can act irrationally in the housing market without making the entire pricing system irrational.

Moreover, this book attempts to show that individuals and companies involved in the housing market can each act rationally and in their own self-interest, yet overvalued home prices can still result. As we will see, this is because the housing market as it is structured today is not a true economic market, and therefore prices can be enormously distorted relative to available information.

Finally, the book would not be complete if it did not offer some advice as to what homeowners can do to protect themselves from an impending downturn in housing prices. This is not as easy as it might sound, as I am sure there are few readers, regardless of how convincing they find our arguments, who will be ready to tell the spouse and kids that they just read a great new book, so it's time to pack up the Chevy and move into a rental apartment. Our challenge is to find other alternatives for the faint of heart that will protect you without so disturbing your family and home.

I hope you find the book informative. People who write such books are sometimes criticized for scaring people or partly contributing to a crash. If I am right, this book is not the problem; it is the solution. The problem is a housing market system in desperate need of reform, reform that should occur now before the situation gets worse.

I would like to thank my publisher, McGraw-Hill, who recognized the serious and timely nature of this text and set a modern-day record in getting this book into print in less than three months. I would specifically like to thank Jeffrey Krames, my editor, and Laura Libretti, both of McGraw-Hill, who were both wonderful to work with and to which this book owes its life.

I would also like to thank my family and friends. My parents, who never said I was overreaching when I talked about my goals while growing up, and my brother and sisters, who often thought I was overreaching but kept it to themselves. I could not have attempted such a task without my friends at UCLA's Anderson School of Management—Dick Roll, my coauthor on our academic papers and my biggest supporter; Ed Leamer, head of the UCLA Forecast and an important contributor to my knowledge of home prices; and Bob Geske, Bhagwan Chowdhry, Robert Spich, Al Osbourne, and Dean Willison for their overall support and encouragement. Their agreement with my thesis is neither expressed nor implied, but my appreciation and thanks to them are both expressed and implied.

Introduction

I have a friend named Frank, who is single, 33 years old, and lives in San Diego, California. (While Frank is a hypothetical person, the incidents described here are drawn from those of a very real person and his actual experiences in recently refinancing his home.) About two years ago, Frank tired of writing rent checks to his landlord and decided to buy a condominium apartment. He paid $195,000 for a two-bedroom apartment with 840 square feet, about 5 minutes from downtown San Diego and 10 minutes from the ocean. I use the word *paid,* but actually, he put up only $4000 of his own money; the rest he borrowed from the bank in the form of a first mortgage. He was a little nervous at the time because two to three years previously similar units in the complex had sold for $140,000.

Last month, Frank decided to refinance his mortgage in order to consolidate his debts and save money, given that mortgage rates had dropped to 6 percent. A mortgage banker handled all the paperwork and the negotiations with the banks. Based on what similar condominiums were selling for in the neighborhood, the mortgage banker was able to find an appraiser who said Frank's unit was now worth $300,000. The banker was able to structure only $240,000 of the loan as a mortgage (because it had to be less than 80 percent of the appraised value to qualify for the attractive rate), but he added an additional $15,000 as a straight bank loan payable over 10 years. Frank ended up qualifying for and borrowing $255,000. He used this money to pay off his old mortgage. There was enough left over for Frank to pay off all of his student loans, all of his credit card debt, and the car loan of $35,000 on his Toyota SUV. One of the risks of such a consolidating loan is that it frees up Frank's credit cards for even bigger borrowings in the future. Although Frank's total debt went up, thanks to lower interest rates and making longer-term loan commitments, Frank was able to lower his overall monthly payments, including property taxes and condo-association fees.

Now, Frank is not a wealthy man. He is one of the good people out there who when given the opportunity to make the big bucks by selling out his soul, decided instead to become a high school teacher. In San Diego, as in the rest of the United States, there is not a lot of money in teaching, especially when one is starting out like Frank. Frank's teaching salary is about $42,000 per year, which he supplements with another $3000 by coaching high school basketball and baseball.

The mortgage bankers were comfortable lending Frank $255,000 based on this total compensation package of $45,000. This represents a ratio of debt to income of approximately 5.7, an aggressive ratio, but not unlike what many Americans are being offered today in their respective cities by equally aggressive mortgage bankers.

But this ratio does not tell the whole story. Frank, like the rest of us, has to pay taxes. Even with the interest deductibility he will enjoy on his mortgage, adding up his taxes—federal, state, and local income taxes, property taxes, and unemployment and disability taxes—means that Frank will owe total taxes of $10,000 this year. Frank's total after-tax income therefore will only be $35,000. Based on this after-tax income, Frank's debt-to-income ratio climbs to 7.3 times his expected after-tax income.

Like the rest of us, Frank has minimum budget requirements for essentials such as food and clothing, utilities, and transportation. If we assume that essential, nondiscriminatory spending for Frank's food and other necessities represents another $12,000, that leaves only $23,000 for Frank's mortgage payments and condo association fees. Under the new mortgage, with its attractive new rates, these payments work out to approximately $1500 per month, or $18,000 per year. This means Frank will have approximately $5000 a year to entertain himself and his girlfriend and try to keep gas in his SUV.

More disturbingly, if we look at Frank's debt ratio in terms of his real after-tax free cash flow of $23,000, his debt ratio has ballooned to over 11 times his real free cash flow.

Ratios of debt to cash flow are probably not something the typical reader will have much familiarity with. It is a shorthand method of telling how leveraged a venture, project, company, or individual is—that is, how much debt it has. Such ratios are very familiar to people on Wall Street doing leveraged buyouts (LBOs). A leveraged buyout simply loads on the maximum amount of debt that a company can tolerate in the hopes that management can buy the company with the borrowed moneys and repay the debt over time, thus making them fabulously wealthy.

To put Frank's debt ratio of 11 in perspective, please realize that most successful LBOs, and by successful I mean those that didn't go bankrupt, were completed at debt ratios of between 3 and 6. At the end of the eighties, when the LBO market imploded, transactions were getting done in the range of 7 to 12 times cash flow, but many of these transactions ended in bankruptcy.

So how could bankers be willing to extend so much money to Frank based on his teacher's salary? Surely, Frank's income is not more stable than some of the companies that went private through leveraged buyouts. Surely, Frank's credit is not as good as some of the LBO borrowers such as GE Credit and Kohlberg, Kravis, Roberts & Co. (KKR). No, regardless of how good a coach Frank is, and regardless of how well his teams do or his students perform, there is a very real risk that Frank may lose his job in the future and with it the ability to service his mortgage payments.

The mortgage lender's assumptions must be threefold. One, if Frank loses his job he will be able to find another job with similar earnings power fairly quickly. Two, the housing prices in San Diego will remain remarkably stable, or increase, so that if Frank had to, he could, easily and quickly, sell his condo and repay his mortgage debt in full. Three, if the bank has to foreclose on Frank, the real estate market will allow the bank to resell the unit for at least the amount of the loan balance.

So, to a great degree, Frank and the lenders are depending on housing prices increasing, or at least remaining stable, for the near future. This certainly has been the case historically as housing prices in San Diego, and in the rest of the country, have continued to escalate to new yearly highs. In this book, we ask whether this will necessarily be true in the future.

You don't need to read a book to know that housing prices are high, in almost every corner of America. The challenge in analyzing home prices is to be able to tell whether the prices are justified by economics or are just floating arbitrarily higher, being driven by some noneconomic forces. Many people refer to such a market as a bubble economy, and then try to explain a combination of psychological and behavioral characteristics of humans that might lead to such "irrational exuberance." I will explore some of these possibilities with regard to housing, but I will return to fundamental economics, thinking to explain the "rational exuberance" inherent in today's housing prices. I do not conclude that the pricing of houses today is rational—just that the prices can be derived assuming that the players in the game are each acting rationally. Frank's actions cannot be deemed irrational as he was very well informed about the housing market and its trends, was of sound mind, and acted much like you or I would have acted under similar circumstances. The lending institution also may have been acting rationally as there is a very small likelihood that this mortgage will ever get on the bank's books. Sometimes, a pricing system has endemic problems in it that prevent it from acting like a true market, and thus allows for some rather unfortunate overvaluations and price distortions.

Finally, I will step back from my theoretical exposition trying to convince you that indeed housing prices may be due for a fall, and direct my attention to practical remedies homeowners and prospective homeowners might take to lessen the pain of any price correction. While not possessing a crystal ball, the reader will hopefully see as he walks through my analysis that the times, they are a changin'.

PART I

THE COMING CRASH IN THE HOUSING MARKET

1

Housing Prices Certainly Look Awfully High

A National Phenomenon

The first three rules of real estate are expressed as "location, location, and location." Real estate is inherently a local business because the value of real estate directly correlates with regional economies and regional demographics. Specific metropolitan home real estate markets also have their own unique market characteristics, and these are examined in Chapter 6. But the present chapter and most of the book look at the United States home real estate market in its entirety.

The reason for such a national analysis, which would seem to violate the above three rules of real estate, is that there are systemic problems in the way that home prices are determined, and these systemic problems are national, if not international, in scope. Although each region of the country has its own unique issues with regard to its economic outlook and home valuations, the nation shares a common methodology for pricing and financing real estate. An inherent problem in the system could affect all areas of the country, albeit to varying degrees. In addition, mortgage interest rates are national, so if they are contributing to a possible overvaluation, the effect would be expected to hold nationwide.

Unless you dwell under a rather large rock, you probably already know that home prices in the United States have been increasing for some time now. The magnitude of the increase (see Figure 1.1) is indeed startling. Median housing prices for existing home sales in the United States increased eightfold over the past 35 years. For newly built homes, the increase is even greater, mostly due to the ever-larger homes being built today. This book focuses primarily on existing home prices because they have more stable year-to-year physical characteristics, and the price comparisons have more applicability, as very few readers actually live in brand-new homes.

This price change in median housing prices for existing homes represents a compound percentage increase of approximately 6.3 percent per year. Almost as striking as the magnitude of the increase is that there has never been a down year during the period. In no year during the last 34 did housing prices decline, year to year. With a historical record like that, it is understandable how someone might come to the conclusion that home real estate is a very good, low-risk investment. There is nothing irrational about using historical experience in making predictions about the future. We do it every day when we assume the sun will rise each morning in the east because it always has in the past.

Figure 1.2 shows that this phenomenon is not restricted to any one region of the country. Although the West has experienced the greatest increases in average home prices with prices increasing nearly tenfold in the period, all regions have shown spectacular price appreciation. The Midwest is the laggard with prices increasing a "measly" sevenfold. These figures support the argument that the appreciation we need to explain is a national, not a regional, issue.

Perhaps anecdotal evidence will help put this in perspective. *Fortune* magazine (October 28, 2002) reports that there was a single three-bedroom, two-bath home in San Francisco that listed for sale, and sold, in 1996 for $285,000. In 2002, it was relisted for sale at an astounding $1,195,000! This is a price appreciation of over 300 percent in just six years. Houses are not like companies. They do not have dramatically increasing earnings due to the creativity of their employees or patents on their inventions. The earning power of a house is fairly consistent: the rent that you can earn on the house pretty much moves slightly up

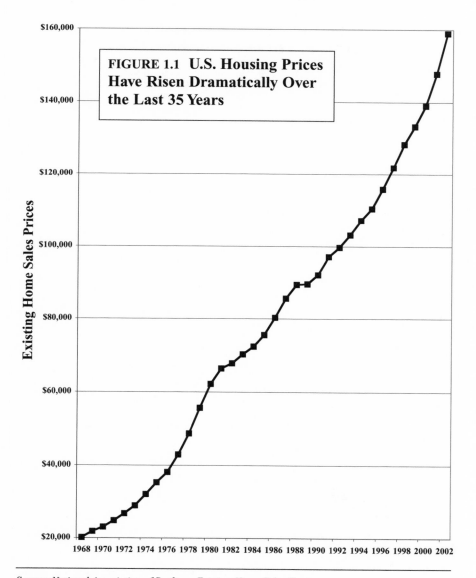

FIGURE 1.1 U.S. Housing Prices Have Risen Dramatically Over the Last 35 Years

Source: National Association of Realtors, Existing Home Sales Survey

or down with the general economy. How can the house price move 300 percent if the underlying rental earnings stream is moving only 2 to 3 percent a year?

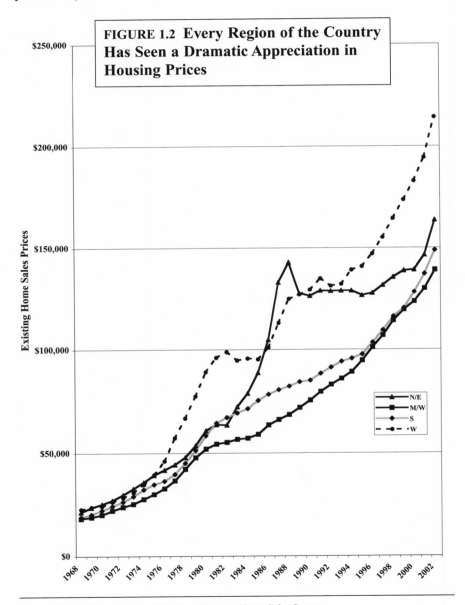

FIGURE 1.2 Every Region of the Country Has Seen a Dramatic Appreciation in Housing Prices

Source: National Association of Realtors, Existing Home Sales Survey

How High Is High?

It is not enough to say that real estate prices are high. We need to do further analysis to ask how high they actually are. *High,* by definition, is a relative term, so in the next chapter we will look at different measures of how high home prices are in relation to other economic statistics. Here we want to see how high they are with regard to where they have been historically. Just because homes are at an all-time high price does not necessarily mean that they are overvalued, but it is an important piece of information to consider in drawing such a conclusion. For example, it would be much harder to argue that home prices were overvalued if a historical analysis showed that they were currently priced at an all-time low. Again, they might still be overvalued under this scenario, but you would have to conclude they were probably even more overvalued in the past. Given the straight upward launch shape of Figure 1.1, no such issue exists here.

A proper analysis of historical home prices should adjust for the effects of general inflation and allow for any changes in the housing stock over time. General inflation is often misunderstood by the public, and sometimes by economic pundits in the media. General inflation occurs when all goods in an economy, on average, increase in price. As you might guess, this should be impossible. However, it does turn out to be possible with the assistance of the Federal Reserve. In order for all goods to increase in price, on average, the Federal Reserve must print more money. The reason that a federal government would print money is pretty obvious—because it can. If we did it, it would be considered counterfeiting. The federal government does it during periods of big government deficits when it needs to pay its bills but doesn't want to raise taxes or go further into debt.

In order to see the "real" price increases in the housing industry over time, we must subtract out that portion of the increase due to general inflation. We would not want to conclude that home prices were really increasing if indeed all goods and services in the economy were increasing by a similar amount. What is important is how housing prices have done relative to other goods and services. This is typically accomplished by translating all prices into a constant dollar measure; here we measure all prices in 2002 dollars. Again, this is usually done by creating a price index like the Consumer Price Index (CPI) and adjusting all prices by how much general prices, measured by the CPI, change year to year. Because the CPI has a shelter, or housing, component that makes up 31 percent of the index, it is more appropriate for our purposes here to use an inflation index that excludes the shelter component. It would be an error if we deflated our housing prices by an index that itself included housing prices. By excluding housing from the index we arrive at prices that are a measure of how housing prices changed over time relative to all other consumption goods other than shelter.

Figure 1.3 shows the prices of housing in 2002 constant dollars after adjusting for general inflation. These "real prices" reflect consumer preference changes over time, to show that consumers value housing more highly in real terms above other consumption goods. Inflation increases are not considered "real" because they say nothing about preferences in choosing between goods. They do not connote real returns on investment, because any inflation dollars received in profits would be squandered in increased prices for consumption goods in the future.

While Figure 1.3 is much less visually dramatic than Figure 1.1, even after adjusting for inflation, home prices have seen a real increase of over 70 percent during the period. It is true that homes, on average, have increased in size during this period. Although no statistics have been kept for existing homes, we know that the square footage of new homes has increased 46 percent during this period, going from 1385 square feet to 2030 square feet, on average. In 2002, the average existing home had a square footage of 1737 square feet. Therefore, we would estimate that the existing homes presented in Figure 1.3 probably increased approximately 25 to 35 percent in square footage. This would mean that approximately half of the real price increase during the period might be explained by the average home's increase in size. While price per square foot typically is a good measure at any particular point in time, nothing says that prices per square foot should be a stable measure over time. For example, couples today buying their first home might more highly value the square footage of a smaller starter home than the price per square foot implied by a McMansion-sized home.

In addition there is an argument that newer homes are of a higher quality than homes of yesteryear and therefore deserve a higher price. It is a fact that many more homes being built today have central air-conditioning, more have garages and fireplaces, and many have a second or third bath. Again, these additions to newly built homes take some time before they affect the average characteristics of all existing homes.

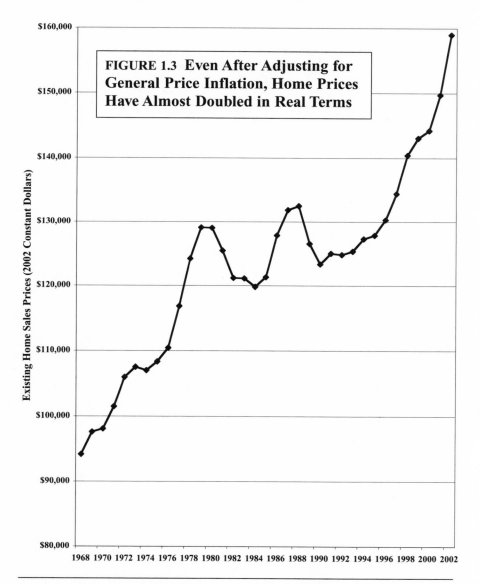

FIGURE 1.3 Even After Adjusting for General Price Inflation, Home Prices Have Almost Doubled in Real Terms

Source: National Association of Realtors, Existing Home Sales Survey; Bureau of Labor Statistics for CPI-U Deflator Without Shelter Costs

You should also consider the other side of the argument. First, today's newly built homes do not seem to be built as soundly as older homes. Steel flooring joists and metal wall studs cause floors to have greater deflections and an unstable feeling and create walls that are less than soundproof. It is not clear that today's quickly built homes reflect the care and pride that craftsmen had in earlier times. Second, homes being built in most crowded metropolitan areas today are farther from downtown, with increased traffic congestion, and longer commute times. Finally, as our public school system has deteriorated, it is natural to assume that the ticket of admission to those schools, namely home ownership in the school district, might also have deteriorated in value.

When Is a Home Not a Home?

There is one further adjustment that can be made to the historical home prices to get a better feel of what has happened to the real prices of homes. It turns out that when you purchase a home you are really buying two distinct assets. One is the physical house that we are all very familiar with. It acts as shelter, but also as the organizing foundation for your family, friends, teachers, clergy, and neighbors, as they all seem to congregate in your kitchen. It is hard to imagine a more important asset in your portfolio.

In addition, when you purchase a home in America, you also purchase a second financial asset, a tax-avoidance scheme. Because interest expense on a mortgage on a primary residence is tax deductible, by purchasing a home with a mortgage you are also creating a tax shield on future income. This shield has real value, in addition to the value of the physical house. Clearly, someone who has mortgage payments of $700 per month is better off than someone who rents a similar place for the same monthly payment. The reason is that homeowners can deduct their interest expense from their taxes and thus pay significantly less income tax than renters.

What is the value of such a deduction over time? We will not go into great detail as to the economic calculation, but suffice it to say that in periods of high inflation and high mortgage rates, the value of this deductibility of interest expense can be quite high, as much as 30 percent of the value of the home in some cases. While the tax advantages increase as mortgage rates increase, they are not so substantial as to prompt the homeowner to wish for higher real rates. Real interest rates are that portion of the nominal rate after subtracting the implied future expected inflation rate. But if the mortgage rate is high because of inflation, it is not a real rate of interest, and yet the tax break is very real. It is during periods of high inflation that this tax avoidance asset has its greatest value. The exact value of this tax advantage is dependent on the price of the home, the income tax bracket of the buyer, the mortgage rate of interest, the expected inflation rate, and the buyer's alternative uses for his or her capital.

Figure 1.4 is a graph of how important this tax avoidance value can be relative to the total purchase price of a home. As you can see, back in the early eighties, when inflation and interest rates topped 15 percent,

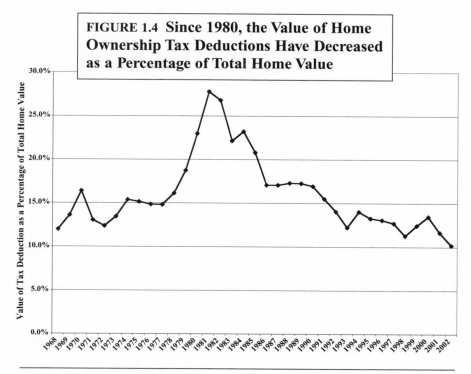

FIGURE 1.4 Since 1980, the Value of Home Ownership Tax Deductions Have Decreased as a Percentage of Total Home Value

Source: National Association of Realtors, Existing Home Sales Survey; Bureau of Labor Statistics for CPI-U Deflator Without Shelter Costs

the value of the tax deduction reached its maximum of nearly 30 percent of the price of the home. As inflation and rates have declined over the past two decades, the relative importance of this deduction has declined substantially. Today, an estimated 10 percent of the price of a new home is due to the tax advantages of home ownership.

If this is the case, why is this tax avoidance asset so important to our understanding of house prices? The reason is that if the value of the tax avoidance asset is declining, and the total purchase price of homes on the market is increasing, then it must be that the price of the underlying physical house asset that we are buying is accelerating at an even greater rate than we previously realized.

In Figure 1.5 you see a plot of the value over time of the pure physical house after subtracting out the value of the tax avoidance asset and after adjusting for inflation. Notice that the value of the pure physical house has been increasing steadily since 1980, and at a faster rate than the combined total price of the house and the tax advantage.

To see this more clearly, look at Figure 1.6. Here, we have plotted the total purchase price of homes, which includes the tax advantage, and a second line, which excludes the tax advantage. We have indexed both lines to 100 to make percentage comparisons easier. You can see that the total purchase price appears to be increasing only since 1995, while the real underlying house asset has been increasing in price almost consistently since 1981. Also, note that the pure house asset has appreciated nearly 60 percent during the 20-year period while the total purchase price, including the tax avoidance scheme, has only increased less than 30 percent. Optimists may see this as evidence that a housing investment looks very good from a historical perspective; the pessimist may be concerned that what goes up must come down.

Conclusion

We have looked at housing prices from a long-term historical perspective. Because housing stock characteristics change over time we cannot definitely conclude that housing is overvalued today. All we can say is that relative to historical prices, today's prices, on a real basis after adjusting for inflation and tax advantages, appear to be at an all-time high. We have not yet done enough analysis to say whether that price can be justified economically.

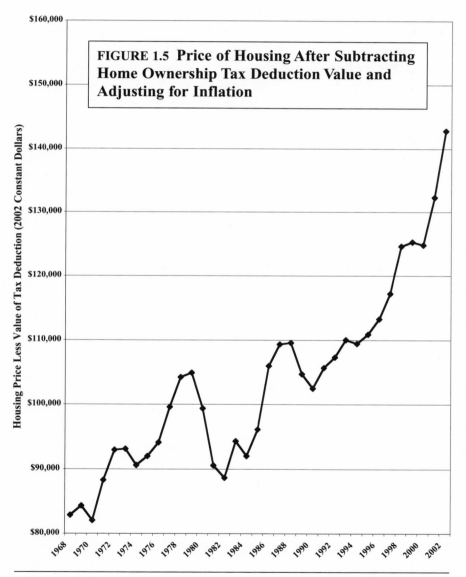

FIGURE 1.5 Price of Housing After Subtracting Home Ownership Tax Deduction Value and Adjusting for Inflation

Source: National Association of Realtors, Existing Home Sales Survey; Bureau of Labor Statistics for CPI-U Deflator Without Shelter Costs

To help us in that endeavor we have to look more closely at the market's more recent experience. See Chapter 2. Focusing on the last three years will be extremely helpful as the housing stock did not change very much over that short time period. The square footage and number of fireplaces per household are probably also similar year to year. Inflation was very low and stable during this period so general inflation and tax advantages of ownership will not muck up the analysis. We also want to look at relative measures other than just historical prices in an attempt to judge whether housing prices are indeed overvalued. We will look at housing prices and begin to compare them to other economic measures such as incomes and rents. Then we will be in a much stronger position to determine if housing is indeed overvalued and headed for a crash.

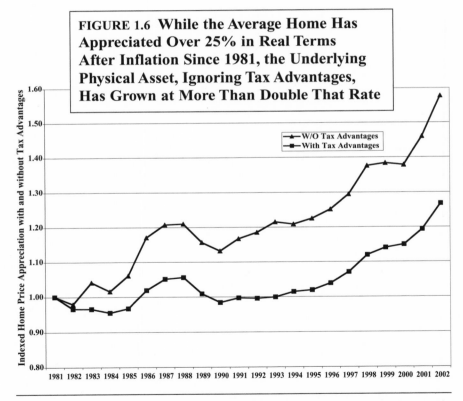

FIGURE 1.6 While the Average Home Has Appreciated Over 25% in Real Terms After Inflation Since 1981, the Underlying Physical Asset, Ignoring Tax Advantages, Has Grown at More Than Double That Rate

Source: National Association of Realtors, Existing Home Sales Survey; Bureau of Labor Statistics for CPI-U Deflator Without Shelter Costs

Summary of Chapter 1

- Housing prices are high across the nation with all regions showing dramatic historical appreciation.
- Nationwide, housing prices have risen eightfold since 1968.
- Even after adjusting for general price inflation in the economy, housing prices have increased 70 percent during this period.
- Half of this increase may possibly be explained by the fact that homes are approximately a third larger today.
- The real price increase in physical housing assets since 1980 is even greater than that stated, because the value associated with the tax deductibility of mortgage interest inherent in the home's overall purchase price has declined over the period as inflation has diminished.

2

High Relative to What?

All Values Are Relative

By definition, judgments of value are always relative. If there were one published national real estate appraisal for every home in the country that everybody could agree on, we could then definitely say that a particular housing market was over- or undervalued. In housing, this is not the case. As a matter of fact, this is not the case in any area of economics.

When we say that a stock's price looks high we mean that it looks high relative to its historical price, or relative to its earnings, or in comparison with other companies in its industry, or even in comparison with theoretically correct values from an academic pricing model. The more agreement there is that a particular model is correct, the greater likelihood that we can reach consensus as to when assets look overvalued, and the greater our surprise when we find that our academic model did not accurately reflect reality.

In engineering school, I flunked a test because my answer was numerically correct, but I had moved the decimal point accidentally one place to the left. When I asked the professor why he had flunked me when my math work and methodology were obviously correct, he said, "John, you don't understand. The bridge you designed just fell down."

Similarly, regardless of how beautiful some of the valuation models are that economists create, if they don't do a good job of explaining reality, their clients will lose their shirts and the "bridge will fall down." We have all heard of the scientist who when told that the experimental predictions from his model did not fit observations in the real world replied, "Well, then we must change reality."

I tell you this because to date there is no really good model for valuing home real estate. Probably the most detailed work is done by individual buyers and their agents when looking at purchasing a particular home. Because we do not know all of the theoretical components to valuing a home, such analysis puts great weight on what similar homes in the neighborhood have sold for recently. This is a fine method for valuation if indeed market prices of homes are good indicators of their inherent long-term value. As we shall see in Chapter 4, this is a very good assumption for most economic markets, but is the housing market a good example of a real economic market?

Therefore, in asking the question as to whether the housing market is overvalued, it is important to continue our work to see relatively how high current housing prices appear. We begin by looking in more detail at how housing prices have moved in the last three years relative to other markets and socioeconomic fundamentals.

Housing Prices Relative to the Economy and the Stock Market

Figure 2.1 is a plot of housing prices relative to recent movements of the stock market and to changes in consumer confidence. All values are indexed to unity so that percentage changes since the beginning of 2000 can be calculated easily.

As can be seen from the graph, home prices have increased approximately 20 percent in value during the period from January 2000 to September 2002, while the Dow Jones Industrial Index has declined 30 percent. The loss in the S&P 500 Index, a broader index incorporating many more companies, has been even worse, declining some 42 percent. Finally, the Consumer Confidence Index has declined by more than half over the period.

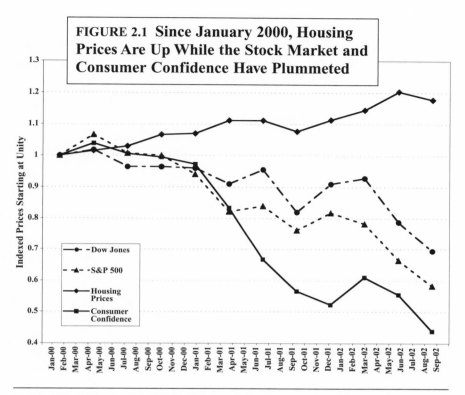

FIGURE 2.1 Since January 2000, Housing Prices Are Up While the Stock Market and Consumer Confidence Have Plummeted

Source: National Association of Realtors, Existing Home Sales Survey; Dow Jones and S&P Indexes, from C&S Trading

Some might argue that such market measures are not "real," that they only measure financial virtual wealth and have no bearing to the real world. To the extent that stock prices are related to future earnings, these stock indexes movements usually foretell very real consequences. The declining prices of these companies are telling us that the market expects these companies to earn less than previously and therefore their assets should be worth less. It is true that people had very grand and ambitious expectations for American companies' earnings and growth in 1999, and a significant percentage of the decline in stock prices can be seen as a realistic adjustment from those lofty aspirations. But there is also evidence that the economy is having real difficulties. The consumer confidence numbers are an indicator of that, but there are also hard economic data available now that the economy is very soft.

The growth in the economy has stalled and our government has gone from a trillion dollar surplus to a trillion dollar deficit position in less than one year. The story at the state level is even worse. In California, we turned an $11 billion surplus into a $35 billion deficit in less than one year, and this on a total budget of only $86 billion. We did have help from the Texas energy producers who benefited from the greatest one-time state-to-state transfer of wealth in history as they purposely manipulated our energy markets during our supposed energy crisis.

Figure 2.2 shows that announced layoffs increased in the recession of 2001 and are up again in what appears to be the beginning of a double dip. Job layoffs are the biggest threat to the mortgage market. It is just such traumatic events as job loss, divorce, and unforeseen medical problems that are the major causes of mortgage defaults.

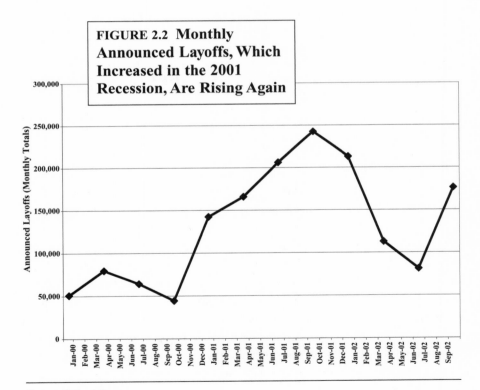

FIGURE 2.2 Monthly Announced Layoffs, Which Increased in the 2001 Recession, Are Rising Again

Source: Federal Reserve

More disturbingly, if housing prices were up, wouldn't you expect other construction activity and other real estate prices to be up also? If housing prices are higher because rates are lower and productive assets are worth more given lower discount rates, wouldn't this translate into higher real estate prices in all areas and greater construction activity in the commercial real estate sector also? Figure 2.3 shows quite clearly that it does not. Nonresidential real estate activity, such as offices, warehouses, and industrial plants, is down while home construction seems to be holding its own. It appears that whatever it is that is driving home prices upward is unique to the housing market.

If part of the value of homeownership is in protecting your loved ones from harm, perhaps home values are increasing because your fam-

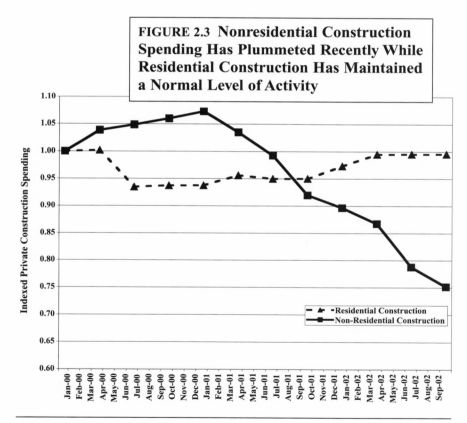

FIGURE 2.3 **Nonresidential Construction Spending Has Plummeted Recently While Residential Construction Has Maintained a Normal Level of Activity**

Source: U.S. Census Bureau

ily is being subjected to higher risks of violence and the purchase of a home is the only means of escape. Possibly, people are willing to pay higher prices for the comfort of knowing their families are safe behind the locked doors and gates of their homes. Figure 2.4 does not support this thesis. As you can see in the figure, crime rates are down across the board. Maybe, looking only at the decline in crime statistics, houses have more value if they are less subject to being vandalized, but I don't believe this accounts for recent housing price increases.

How is it that prices of almost all other assets and stocks are declining, business activity and commercial construction is slowing, the economy is soft, and yet housing prices are on the rise? Maybe people have lost money in their prior investments and are looking for a safe place to put their money. Maybe that's it! Maybe when they pulled their money out of the depressed tech stocks they wanted to put it someplace safe— some investment literally close to home that they really understood.

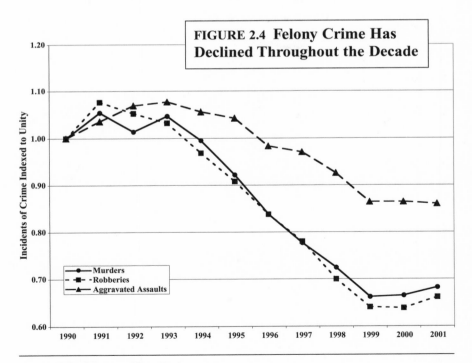

FIGURE 2.4 Felony Crime Has Declined Throughout the Decade

Source: Federal Bureau of Investigation

Something as unlike the ephemeral Internet stocks as possible, a hard asset—bricks and mortar.

I see two problems with this housing investment philosophy. First, to the extent housing prices may be up because of an increased flow of funds into the sector, what happens when that flow slows or reverses? Doesn't there have to be an underlying principle of value that justifies the higher home prices? If supply of funds to a market is the only consideration, than where do home prices go when that supply of investment capital stops?

Second, just because houses are made with bricks and mortar does not necessarily mean that investing in homes is a safe investment. It is true that it is unlikely that houses will suddenly evaporate like so many Internet companies did in the last few years. But the critical question in analyzing an investment is not whether it is composed of bricks and mortar, but rather, what price you paid for those bricks and mortar. At debt ratios exceeding 10 to 1, housing prices need not decline much for one's total investment to be at risk.

The analogy to the stock market comes from my mother. She always liked IBM as a company, thought they had the best people, and agreed with their customer service philosophy. She therefore concluded that it would be a good stock investment. She did not ask the critical question, how high a price or P/E was IBM selling for? My mother likes oranges, but she would never buy any at the store without first looking at their price. Similarly, a beautiful three-bedroom house overlooking the ocean may be a good investment at $500,000, but a terrible investment if priced at $4.6 million.

Housing Prices Relative to Incomes

To further understand these relative measures of price we must extend our analysis beyond just historical prices and alternative markets and begin to understand the fundamentals that drive the value of homes.

One way to measure how relatively high home prices have become is to compare them with household incomes over time. You might expect that home prices as a multiple of incomes would decline over time as households in America became wealthier. In other words, you might expect a population that is getting wealthier to have to spend less of its income on shelter. You might think that technological advances might have made it cheaper to construct homes today as opposed to low-tech yesteryear. You might guess this, but you would be wrong! Figure 2.5 shows just the opposite relationship. Housing prices increased dramatically faster than household incomes in the seventies; the ratio stayed relatively constant for the eighties and nineties and exploded in the last two years. People are devoting more of their income than ever to housing. Figure 2.6 shows that in 2000, the most recent year for which data are available, housing was far and away the dominant expense of most households. Since then, housing prices have continued to increase faster than other household consumption items.

The story is even more dramatic than Figure 2.5 purports. The reason is that today most government housing statistics speak in terms of household incomes. But there has been a dramatic change in the makeup

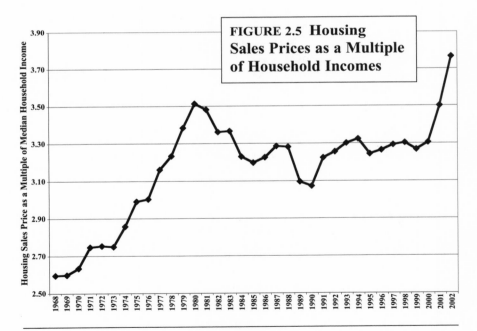

FIGURE 2.5 **Housing Sales Prices as a Multiple of Household Incomes**

Source: National Association of Realtors, Existing Home Sales Survey; Census Bureau, Current Population Survey for Household Incomes

of the wage earners of most households in America over the past 40 years. Figure 2.7 shows that the percentage of women in the workforce has increased from around 30 to over 60 percent during the last four decades. These percentages are very similar for married women who have entered the workforce during this time period. Rather than creating a nest egg for their retirement, money for their children's education, or a cushion against a rainy day, many families are seeing their second incomes eaten up in higher and higher mortgage payments on ever-increasing home prices. Markets can be very cruel at times. It is as if the market watches the extra family income arrive, and then demands it in higher mortgage payments before the family can ever begin to enjoy it.

These pooled household incomes, in which both wage earners' salaries are pledged to pay the home mortgage, introduce another form of risk to the housing market. What happens in divorce? Since both incomes are necessary to cover the mortgage costs, how does one per-

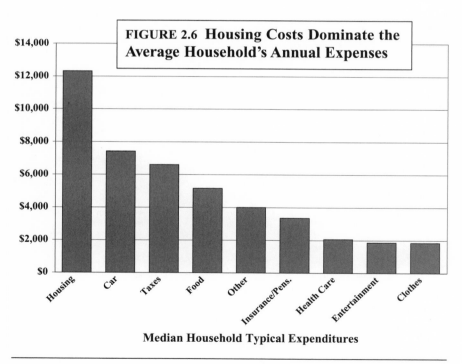

FIGURE 2.6 Housing Costs Dominate the Average Household's Annual Expenses

Median Household Typical Expenditures

Source: U.S. Bureau of Labor Statistics, Consumer Expenditures in 2000

son do it alone? The assumption is that the family moves after a divorce into less expensive shelter, but this assumption also requires that home prices are stable or increasing to facilitate the sale of the family home. We foresee many disgruntled couples remaining married against their better judgment solely to pay off the family mortgage. The math simply does not work if one person keeps the house and kids, and the other has to fund payments on a new place as well as continue to make partial payments on the old house.

It is somewhat enlightening to look at home prices in the old-fashioned way—assuming that there is only one breadwinner in the family, or that only one person's salary should really be tied up in the purchase of a home. This is not an attempt to be chauvinistic. I really don't care if the breadwinner is a man or a woman. I only want to show that the assumption that there will always be two wage earners in a household is a dan-

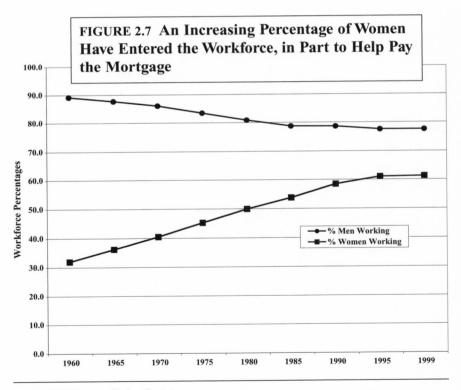

FIGURE 2.7 An Increasing Percentage of Women Have Entered the Workforce, in Part to Help Pay the Mortgage

Source: U.S. Bureau of Labor Statistics

gerous assumption. Figure 2.8 shows what has happened to individual worker's annual wages over time. When we use this single worker model rather than the total household income model previously shown in Figure 2.5, we come up with a distinctly different picture of how high home prices

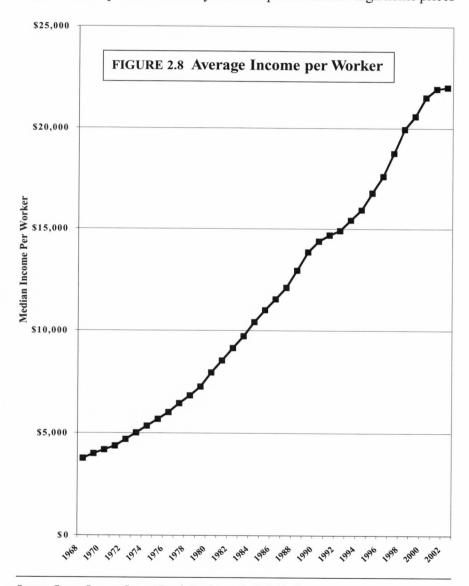

FIGURE 2.8 Average Income per Worker

Source: Census Bureau, Current Population Survey for Individuals

are. Figure 2.9 shows us housing prices as a multiple of the average single worker's income rather than total household income. If home prices are financed with 80 to 90 percent mortgage debt, you can see that the pricing, and therefore the debt ratio, on the individual, is getting very steep.

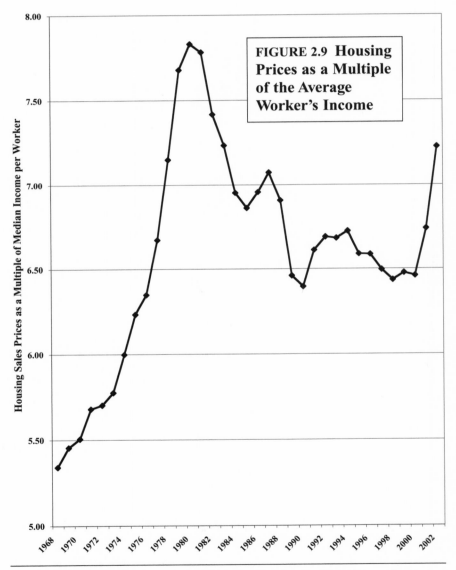

FIGURE 2.9 Housing Prices as a Multiple of the Average Worker's Income

Source: National Association of Realtors, Existing Home Sales Survey; Census Bureau, Current Population Survey for Household Incomes

This is not the full story, however. Again convention allows that we show these debt ratios based on pretax income. If we assume that fully half of a homeowner's pretax income will be consumed in taxes, utilities, and necessities such as minimum amounts of food, clothing, and

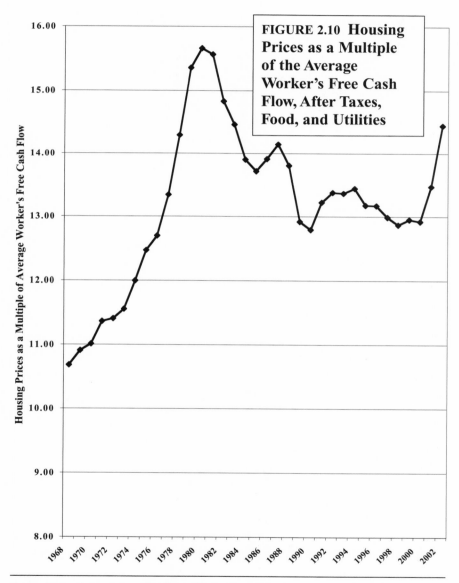

FIGURE 2.10 Housing Prices as a Multiple of the Average Worker's Free Cash Flow, After Taxes, Food, and Utilities

Source: National Association of Realtors, Existing Home Sales Survey; Census Bureau, Current Population Survey for Household Incomes

transportation expense, then the debt ratio to the individual's free cash flow after taxes and essentials is much worse. Figure 2.10 paints this picture. One can see that prices relative to individual incomes are on the rise again and, at an average 14 times free cash flow, are extremely high. Remember, as discussed in this book's introduction, that successful highly leveraged transactions on Wall Street are typically done with debt levels equal to six to eight times the company's free cash flow. (For highly leveraged corporations, pretax income equals after-tax income as the large interest expense means little to no taxes will be due.) Just as a company's cash flow is not certain in the future, the individual worker's job future in an uncertain business environment is uncertain. If 14 is the median average multiple relative to individuals' free cash flows, this means that fully half of all housing transactions involving two wage earners occurring today are being accomplished at ratios exceeding 14 times one wage earner's free cash flow.

Housing Prices Relative to Potential Rental Incomes

While examinations of housing prices relative to household and individuals' incomes are interesting, there is nothing that says that a stable relationship should exist between the two. One could imagine people's incomes increasing tenfold, but construction costs of housing appreciating much more slowly. While the ratio of housing prices to incomes seems to put an upper limit on housing prices due to the debt service that needs to be paid, there is no hard-and-fast rule as to how incomes and house prices should be related.

Ed Leamer of UCLA's Anderson School of Management noted in his recent work as director of the UCLA Anderson Forecast that it is not housing prices to incomes that should have a stable relationship over time, but rather housing prices and comparable rental income. The price you pay for a home should have a fairly fixed relationship to the rental income you could garner if you decided to put the property on the rental market. Simply said, the price of a home must have some relationship to the income that the home is capable of producing. This is the very same concept that says that stock prices must have some relationship to their earnings power. Thus when people talk about how expensive stocks are they talk about how high their P/Es are. Similarly, Professor Leamer asks what housing P/E we are paying for our homes. His definition of a housing P/E is its market price divided by the annual rental income it could generate. If homes trade at prices with very large housing P/Es, homeowners cannot recover their investment through earnings, or rental income, over time. Clearly, if they choose to occupy the house they recoup their investment in other less quantifiable ways, but the best way to measure the value of these softer returns is to understand the opportunity cost of not renting the house for cash.

Professor Leamer has done some interesting work relating home prices to rental incomes in comparing the Los Angeles and San Fran-

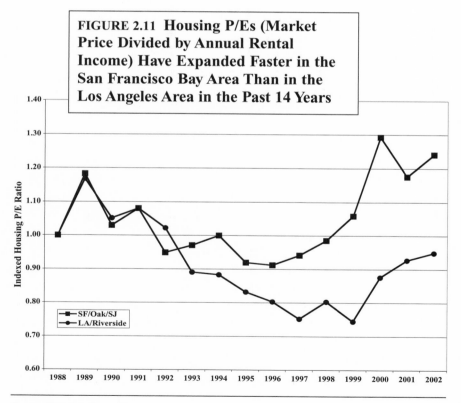

FIGURE 2.11 **Housing P/Es (Market Price Divided by Annual Rental Income) Have Expanded Faster in the San Francisco Bay Area Than in the Los Angeles Area in the Past 14 Years**

Source: UCLA Anderson Forecast

cisco housing markets. Figure 2.11 shows that on an indexed basis, the home P/Es for San Francisco and Los Angeles tracked closely until 1992, at which time the P/E for LA declined relative to the P/E for San Francisco (or San Francisco increased relative to LA). The 30 percent current difference in P/Es is due to the fact that San Francisco housing prices continued to escalate through 2002 even as the rental market softened. Homebuyers in San Francisco are not thinking like investors and are not focused on what their property investment can earn in potential rental income. It is interesting to note that buyers of apartment buildings in San Francisco have seen a decline in apartment building prices as houses continue to rise in price. Apartment building buyers are much more financially savvy than your typical homeowner and look at their real estate investments from a businessperson's perspective. They have cap rates of return that they require from their properties (the inverse of a P/E) and as rents soften they immediately push the market price for apartment buildings lower. We will examine this approach of comparing housing prices to apartment building prices in much more detail when we look at the regional economics of housing later in Chapter 6.

Part of the reason for a decline in rents and an increase in home prices may be an increasing desire on behalf of consumers to own rather than rent. But this desire has always been there. It is much more likely that prospective homeowners are being lured into paying ever-increasing prices for homes because they can. In other words, banks and other lending institutions are giving people more and more money to transact house purchases.

The chief economist at Morgan Stanley, Stephen Roach, said on October 23, 2002, that there were "still a few more bubbles to be popped" in the U.S. economy. Roach warned that there was a very real danger of having the housing bubble burst. "We have the biggest disparity between house prices and rental rates we've ever had, so I think we have a housing bubble," Roach said. Roach also pointed to the 27 percent real increase in home prices since 1997, after accounting for general inflation, the sharpest run-up in home prices in any five-year period since 1945 (UPI–Business and Economics Desk–October 23, 2002). *Fortune* magazine (October 28, 2002) reports that since 1996, U.S. real rents have increased just 10 percent, adjusted for inflation, one-third of the 30 percent jump in housing prices.

Housing Prices Relative to Interest Rates

The preceding discussion brings us to the major reason why home prices have risen so dramatically as of late: low interest rates. Figure 2.12 is a graph of the interest rates over time on 30-year fixed rate mortgages.

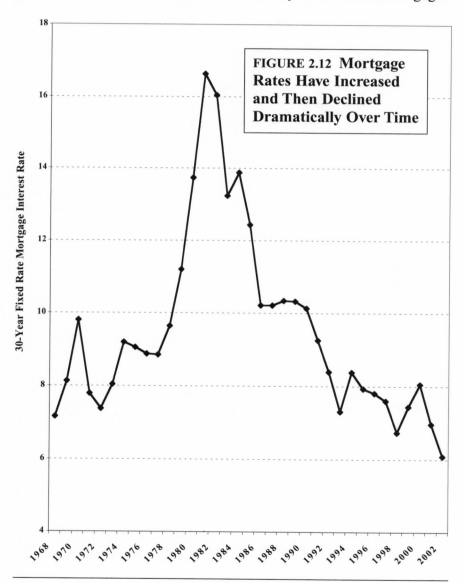

FIGURE 2.12 Mortgage Rates Have Increased and Then Declined Dramatically Over Time

Source: Freddie Mac for 30-Year Fixed Interest Rate Mortgages

Peaking above 16 percent in 1981, they have declined precipitously and now stand at around 6 percent. You could argue that Leamer's home P/Es should expand somewhat in a reduced interest rate environment as the rental income stream can be discounted at a smaller real discount rate, meaning that productive assets should be valued more highly. But for this to be true you would have to believe that the rate decline is permanent.

Lower rates directly impact housing prices because banks and mortgage brokers all use essentially the same formula to determine the amount of funding that a family qualifies for. The biggest determinates in this formula are twofold, family income and mortgage rates.

Unfortunately, we will see that many of the lenders who are applying this formula do not ask the basic question: what happens if rates rise in the future? While the individual homeowner may have fixed his rate for 30 years, the effect of an interest rate rise on the housing construction market, on housing prices, and on the general economy has never been fully explored. Through no fault of his own, the homeowner may find himself stuck in a house whose market value may not even equal the total mortgage debt on it. In Chapter 3, we will take a look at how leveraged with debt the average American family is and what that means about the family's ability to weather a housing price downturn.

Summary of Chapter 2

- All values are relative.
- No good model exists for valuing homes other than neighborhood appraisals that focus solely on current "market values" of similar properties.
- In the last couple of years, the economy has softened, layoffs are up, the stock market is down, consumer confidence is down dramatically, office construction is down, threatening crime is down, and yet housing prices are up.
- Housing prices relative to household incomes are up.
- Household incomes now include the earnings power of about 60 percent of married women who work, up from just 30 percent in 1960, and yet housing prices have risen faster than these two–wage-earner households on a combined income basis.

- If housing prices are examined relative to a single worker's income rather than the entire household's income, then prices look awfully high.
- Housing in many metropolitan areas is also increasing in price faster than potential rental income. Known as a housing P/E, such a divergence cannot be sustained in the long term.
- The recent interest rate decline explains much of the house appreciation, but begs the question: Are rates always going to be this low?

3

How Much Debt Do You Have?

The Housing Market Is Built on Leverage

We shall see that what makes an asset-based market like the home housing market risky is the sheer volume of the leverage, or the debt, in the system. Leverage is simply how much debt individuals and institutional players in the system carry against their assets. It is called leverage, or borrowing, because it leverages, or increases, the potential returns from an investment. A 5 percent return on an asset becomes a 50 percent return to equity capital if leveraged with nine dollars of debt for every one dollar of equity (ignoring for now the cost of the debt).

Because there is no free lunch in economics, the increased return potential is matched by an increased risk profile. The investor can easily turn any relatively safe asset like property into a risky investment by layering on debt. A rather safe income stream from the unleveraged asset can become a net income stream after interest expense that is much more volatile, unpredictable, and risky.

Why would individuals wish to create such a risky asset? The answer is that the upside potential is enormous. If you had bought an average home in 1968 for the median average price of $20,000 available at the time, and only put down $2000, or 10 percent, of the purchase price, your profit from selling in September 2002 would have been $140,000 (again for simplicity we ignore borrowing costs here, a reasonable assumption if you rent the property out and the rent covers the mortgage payments). This is a profit equal to 70 times your original $2000 investment or 10 times what it would have been without the use of leverage.

So individuals should not be relied upon to limit their debt exposure, especially in highly leveraged financings like home mortgages, where the individual may view his investment as an option on higher real estate prices. Volatility and price appreciation are his friends as they both increase the value of his option, and therefore, the more leverage the better. Option theory predicts that buyers may try to buy the most expensive home possible, as this will give them control of the largest possible option contract.

If the individual is not motivated to control his debt leverage then it must fall to the lenders to act as the debt police in such transactions. We will see that the lenders are also not very motivated to act as a damper on debt, either for the homeowner or for themselves.

Many Homeowners Are Highly Leveraged

Figure 3.1 shows what has happened to total domestic borrowing in our nation over time. Clearly we have become a citizenry rather addicted to credit. It comes in many forms: first and second mortgages, auto loans, student loans, credit card debt, home improvement loans, home equity loans, and general revolving loans. We seem to like all of them. As of 1999, the average owner-occupied residence was approximately $80,000 in debt, including the mortgage, while renter-occupied homes were approximately $22,000 in debt. Mortgage loans are by far the biggest market with over $5.7 trillion of mortgage debt outstanding as of today. Remember, the entire United States government has only $6.3 trillion of debt outstanding. A trillion here, and a trillion there, and pretty soon we are talking real money.

How does this leverage relate to the typical homeowner? Figure 3.2 shows that the average new homeowner is using more and more debt to cover the purchase price of his home. Only in recent years has there been any decline in this debt-to-value percentage, and that was probably unintentional as home prices grew faster than financing arrangements could keep up. Remember, these are median averages. If the average debt-to-value percentage peaked at 80 percent, that means half of the people had mortgage debt in excess of 80 percent of their purchase prices.

The increase in debt can be seen in the next chart, Figure 3.3, which tracks the percentage of homebuyers who have put down less than 10 percent of the total purchase price over the past 30 years. Peaking at 27 percent in 1983 and again in 1995, the proportion is still a relatively high 20 percent today. These are the people most at risk if housing prices go down. If housing prices decline by just 11 percent, these homeowners are living in an underwater asset—that is, the market value will not be sufficient to pay off the debt if a sale is required. The number of people in this situation has greatly expanded over the last few years. Many homeowners have taken advantage of the low rate environment to refinance their mortgages and run their total debt back above 90 percent of the home's market value.

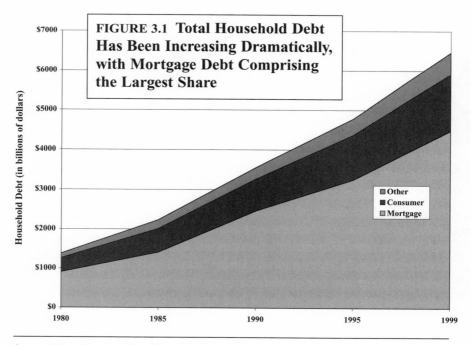

FIGURE 3.1 Total Household Debt Has Been Increasing Dramatically, with Mortgage Debt Comprising the Largest Share

Source: Federal Reserve, Flow of Funds

Figure 3.4 is designed to show that, cumulatively, 20 million households in America spend more than 40 percent of their total household
income on housing costs and that 10 million of these households spend
more than 80 percent of their income on housing costs. These data

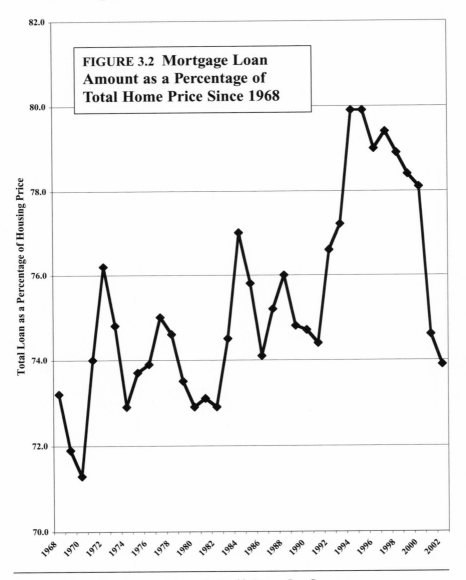

Source: U.S. Federal Housing Finance Board, Monthly Interest Rate Survey

include renters as well as homeowners, but it does say something about how expensive shelter in our country has become and how tightly people have drawn the line regarding housing expenses.

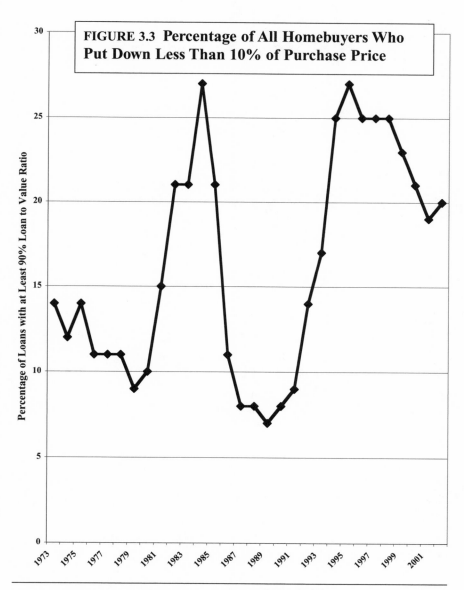

FIGURE 3.3 **Percentage of All Homebuyers Who Put Down Less Than 10% of Purchase Price**

Source: U.S. Federal Housing Finance Board, Monthly Interest Rate Survey

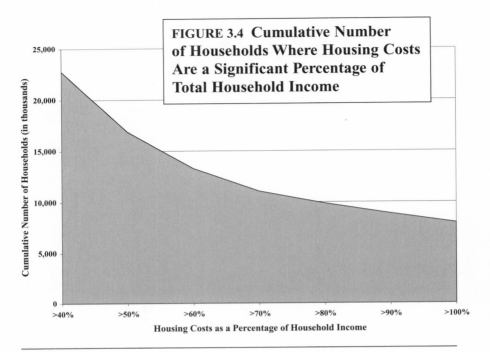

FIGURE 3.4 **Cumulative Number of Households Where Housing Costs Are a Significant Percentage of Total Household Income**

Source: Census Bureau, American Housing Survey 2001

Figure 3.5 makes this point directly for homeowners by looking at whether an average worker's salary after tax and after necessities like food and clothing could cover the mortgage payments on a hypothetical average house sold in each year. Ratios below 1 mean that the average worker would have defaulted if not for the support of his or her spouse's paycheck, or that the average American in many years could not afford the average house in this country without spousal support.

How big a bet is the typical American making on a house? You can see in Figure 3.6 that the average American's net worth is only $70,000, and that people under 35 have net worths, on average, equal to only $10,000. It is fair to say that most Americans have more equity capital in their homes than in their stock portfolios. Therefore a 20 percent decline in the average home price in this country would not only reduce, on average, people's net worths by half, but would bankrupt many Americans, especially younger Americans.

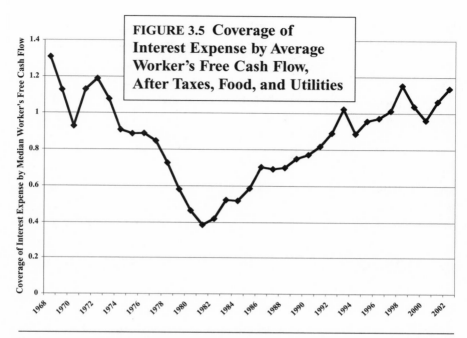

FIGURE 3.5 Coverage of Interest Expense by Average Worker's Free Cash Flow, After Taxes, Food, and Utilities

Source: National Association of Realtors, Existing Home Sales Survey; Census Bureau, Current Population Survey for Household Incomes; Freddie Mac for 30-Year Fixed Rate Mortgages

The Leverage End Game: Foreclosure and Personal Bankruptcy

Probably the most shocking exhibit in this entire book is Figure 3.7, but it needs some explanation. This is a graph of the percentage of mortgages that enter into foreclosure proceedings each quarter. The total in foreclosure today is approximately 1.2 percent of the total mortgage debt outstanding, but as this figure shows, this number is growing rapidly.

What is so shocking about this figure is not the upward slope of an ever-increasing rate of foreclosures. Remember, this is a plot of rates, not levels, so an upward sloping shape to this plot means that foreclosures are not only increasing, but at an ever increasing rate. But this is not the real shock. The really shocking news is that foreclosures would be increasing at all, given that home prices are increasing in value at the fastest pace in history. One would naturally expect this curve to be, not only flat, but declining. Just in the last three years the foreclosure rate has increased 25 percent, but we know that home prices increased 20 percent over these same three years. How can you have the foreclosure rate increasing while housing prices are increasing? Even if the homeowner loses his job or has other troubles in making his mortgage payments, in a strong housing market like this he can always sell his home at a profit and easily pay back the mortgage lender in full.

I think this is the most disturbing trend of all the numbers we have analyzed to date. Here we see the foreclosure rate accelerating rather dramatically in the face of the healthiest and most robust housing market in our history. What will happen if housing prices soften? What if people get in trouble through job losses, but do not have the option of selling their home quickly at a profit in order to repay the banks because home prices are down? We can tell you what will happen to the shape

FIGURE 3.6 Family Net Worth by Age of Head of Household

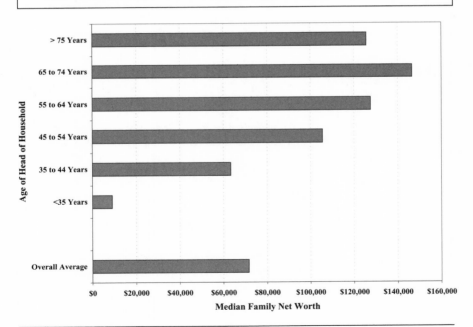

Source: Board of Governors, Federal Reserve System

of this curve. It will no longer be a smooth upward sloping linear curve. There will be a big disconnect and the rate of foreclosures will jump enormously. This is one of the keys to our analysis in this book. Historical experience, especially in default rates and foreclosures, means next to nothing as those events occurred during a period of ever-increasing housing prices and a fairly healthy economy. If housing prices soften, then this type of historical experience is meaningless. And institutions such as banks, mortgage insurance providers, mortgage packagers, mortgage investors, and others that are depending on a historical default rate continuing into the future are about to be rudely awakened. More about this later, in Chapter 9.

On November 24, 2002, the *New York Times* reported that mortgage foreclosures were not just a bicoastal phenomenon. Nowhere is the problem of foreclosures worse than in Indiana, where the Mortgage Bankers

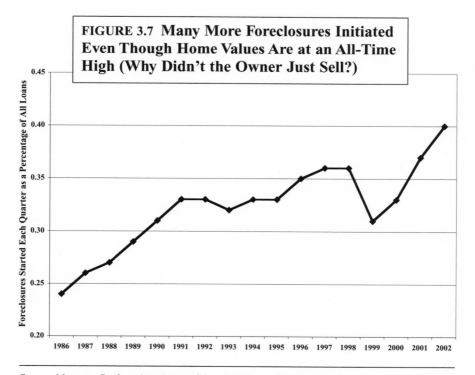

FIGURE 3.7 Many More Foreclosures Initiated Even Though Home Values Are at an All-Time High (Why Didn't the Owner Just Sell?)

Source: Mortgage Bankers Association of America, National Delinquency Survey

Association of America found 2.22 percent of all housing in foreclosure, the highest rate in the country. Foreclosures are highest among so-called sub-prime loans, those higher-rate loans made to people with less than perfect credit ratings. "We're seeing the implications of reduced standards that sub-prime lenders applied. The expectations were that we would see more fail, and now we're seeing them fail," said William Apgar, the federal housing commissioner under Bill Clinton, and now a senior scholar at the Joint Center for Housing Studies at Harvard.

In two big recent settlements to stop sub-prime lenders from taking advantage of homeowners through predatory lending, CitiGroup Inc. agreed in September 2002 to reimburse homebuyers $215 million. Then in October of 2002, Household International agreed to pay up to $484 million as they came under pressure from community groups like ACORN in Illinois concerned about how their members were allegedly getting ripped off by the consumer financing group. Household has recently announced their sale to HSBC, a bank holding company from London, as their consumer lending problems made their own company financing efforts unmanageable. In essence, Household itself had become a sub-prime borrower.

As we said, 1.2 percent of all mortgages are currently in foreclosure. This is just part of the story. As Figure 3.8 demonstrates, the number of personal bankruptcies has exploded over the last 20 years. Topping 1.5 million persons, homeowners make up more than half of this number. The number of homeowners claiming personal bankruptcy has jumped from 450,000 to over 750,000 in just five years. This has occurred as mortgage debt outstanding has jumped 50 percent to almost $5.7 trillion over the last four years.

The *Wall Street Journal* on November 13, 2002, quoted Elizabeth Warren, a Harvard law professor who specializes in consumer bankruptcy, as saying that there is a direct connection between the massive levels of mortgage-related debt and the rise in personal bankruptcies. "I think we're only seeing the front end of this wave," she said. The article reported that nearly one in five homeowners refinanced their mortgages in the past year, with 30 percent of those using some of the proceeds to pay down other debt. Professor Warren calls this an "unmitigated disaster" because it comes on top of ever-increasing amounts of credit card debt.

Not everyone is alarmed by the increasing trend in personal bankruptcies and mortgage foreclosures. Freddie Mac is the second largest purchaser and packager of mortgages and pass-through securities after Fannie Mae. Their chief economist, Frank Nothaft, says that he doesn't see the connection between the increase in personal bankruptcies and increased levels of mortgage borrowings. He blames increasing cultural acceptance of bankruptcy for the problem and thinks that refinancings that pledge people's homes as collateral to repay other debt is the right step for families to take to get out from under burdensome debt.

We will see that part of the problem here, as elsewhere, is that those institutions closest to this issue have the potential to let their narrow self-interest outweigh the public interest. Realtors, mortgage brokers, appraisers, commercial bankers, mortgage insurers, Fannie Mae and Freddie Mac, and even Alan Greenspan all have an interest in preserving confidence in the mortgage system, even if it is broke and in desperate need of fixing. Even Alan Greenspan? Yes, even Alan Greenspan. The reason

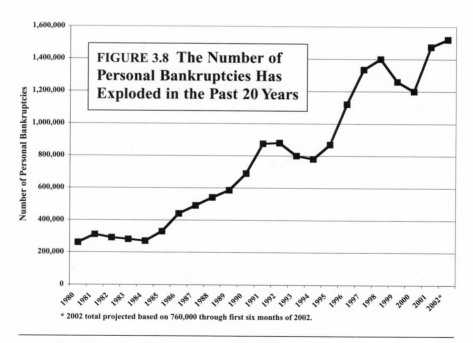

FIGURE 3.8 The Number of Personal Bankruptcies Has Exploded in the Past 20 Years

* 2002 total projected based on 760,000 through first six months of 2002.

Source: Federal Reserve; AOUSC, American Bankruptcy Institute

is that he works for the Federal Reserve Board, which is owned and controlled by the country's commercial banks, which in turn hold plenty of home mortgage assets on their books. In addition, he has his hands full right now with a weak economy and a collapsing stock market. The last thing he needs right now is to have a housing crash. Remember, homeowners' spending of money that they have taken out of their homes through refinancings is one of the few bright spots of the current economy.

Perhaps you are aware of Washington's proposed solution to the increase in personal bankruptcies. Always willing to take the campaign money of the credit card and mortgage industries, Congress has concluded that the solution to the problem of too many bankruptcies is to make it much more difficult for citizens to claim bankruptcy. Specifically, people claiming bankruptcy would not free themselves of older debt obligations if they returned to a positive cash flow position in the near future. So much for giving someone a new start on life. It should give you no comfort that this proposal was recently temporarily defeated in the House. The only reason the banking industry lost is that they were opposed by the antiabortion lobby that wanted to preserve its ability to claim bankruptcy if the civil fines from abortion clinic protests became too much to handle. These are stranger-than-strange opponents, and we can assure you the banking lobby will not let these antiabortion protestors get in the way next time.

The fact is that this "solution" would do nothing to address the underlying cause of the problem. Banks and credit card companies are becoming more and more aggressive in their lending terms. Citibank, at one time in the eighties, rather than do credit analysis to determine if they take on a new credit card customer, decided to avoid most of the paperwork hassle and just mailed valid credit cards to millions of Americans around the country. Enormous bad debt losses resulted. We shall see that the aggressive terms of mortgage lenders is not only endangering the health of the mortgage market, but is also contributing to the unhealthy rise in home prices around the country and presenting a real threat to our country's economic prosperity.

Summary of Chapter 3

- The housing market has enormous amounts of debt leverage throughout the system.
- While debt leverage can dramatically increase returns to homeowners, banks, and quasi-governmental agencies in the mortgage business, it can dramatically increase risk and magnify losses in bad times.
- Homeowners have taken on record amounts of mortgage and consumer debt.
- Mortgage foreclosures are occurring at an increasing rate, which should be surprising given that home prices are escalating and the economy is still doing quite well.
- Personal bankruptcies have reached record levels also.

C H A P T E R

Why a Crash Is Likely

Rational or Irrational Exuberance

This chapter examines whether the participants in the housing market are acting rationally, whether the housing sector qualifies as a real "economic market" to begin with, whether this market appears to be acting rationally with regard to pricing, and whether there is a rational explanation of how home prices could have gotten this high.

Many believe that for a crash in a market to occur, the participants must have been behaving irrationally to begin with to allow prices to get so high. They draw little distinction between irrational participants and irrational markets. When a market appears overvalued, many leap to the conclusion that its participants are acting irrationally, and they ignore the possibility that participants may actually be acting perfectly rationally—that is, while prices appear high relative to history, prices may indeed reflect people's beliefs that the economic good in question is going to be in greater and greater demand in the future and its supply will be limited, thus generating opportunities for increased earnings from the asset. Not all bubbles burst. Some continue to grow into successful companies or entire new industries. Just because prices are high relative to their historical levels does not mean that a bubble exists or that prices are sure to fall in the future.

In times of dramatically higher market prices, others are quick to declare that the market itself is acting irrationally. This is a serious charge to any market economist because it attacks the credibility of all markets. If free markets do not do the best job of assigning prices, then how can they do the best job of allocating resources? And if markets are subject to frequent bubbles and crashes, is a free market system the best system to organize an economy and a society around?

There is a very big difference between charging that some of the participants in a market are acting irrationally and concluding that the market itself is acting irrationally in setting prices. The best example of this occurs at horse racing tracks around the world. Anyone who has attended a horse race can tell you tales of the large number of railbirds at the track who are more than willing to share with you the secrets to their supposed success. Far from being rational, their "winning" strategies include betting on the color of the jockey's silks, the sound of the horse's name, the state where he was bred, the weight he is carrying, or their favorite lucky number.

And yet, out of this chaos, order comes. By the time the race starts, the odds on the tote board are a very good predictor of how the horses will run. Why is this? The reason is twofold. First, the true odds on the tote board are only affected by real bets, not chat along the rail. The odds follow the money. Second, if these odds get out of line with someone's best estimate of the correct odds, he or she can correct them by wagering money on the underpriced entry until the odds come into line and the arbitrage profit opportunity disappears. So here we have a very good example of many irrational participants and a very rational market.

Eugene Fama of the University of Chicago, my morning-line favorite to win the Nobel Prize in economics, has been a big defender of his pathbreaking work on the efficiency of markets. Efficiency is another way of saying that market pricing acts rationally, that all available information is incorporated in the price, and that the price is the best predictor of future opportunities. If markets are efficient, then bubbles should be rare, as prices should not be allowed to overinflate without someone, like the horse bettor at the track, stepping in and profiting from the error and returning the price to normal. Prices can appear relatively high, but it should be impossible to predict in advance whether they will continue ever upward, or will turn and head south. Market efficiency at its simplest says it is impossible to beat the market over the long term.

Mark Rubinstein of the University of California at Berkeley, cocreator of the Cox-Rubinstein option pricing formula, has written an academic paper published in the May/June 2001 issue of the *Financial Analysts Journal* defending the efficient market theory from attack by the behavioral economists. Behavioral economists have come to hold suspect the market's ability to act rationally given the long list of human shortcomings to rationality. Their list of human shortcomings that they believe can affect the rationality of markets is quite lengthy and includes the following: human hubris and overconfidence; the inability of people to assign correct probabilities, especially to very rare events; overreaction, especially to recent or personal experience; people incorrectly dealing with "sunk" costs; people's tendency to gamble or take unnecessary risks; selective recall; and poor self-control.

In the present housing market there appears to be a psychological component, as new homebuyers seem anxious to get in before prices rise to unattainable levels. Figure 4.1 shows that there is indeed a feeding

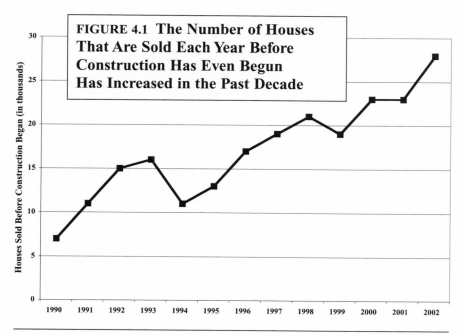

FIGURE 4.1 **The Number of Houses That Are Sold Each Year Before Construction Has Even Begun Has Increased in the Past Decade**

Source: Census Bureau

frenzy on in the current housing market as people are buying an increasing number of homes that have not even started construction at the time of the sale.

Eugene Fama, in a research paper published in the September 1998 issue of the *Journal of Financial Economics,* points out that approximately half of the behaviorists' theories suggest that prices are overstated while the other half predict understated prices, so on average, and considering that none of their price biases is large, the net result is that the market might indeed be pricing correctly.

Rubenstein argues that if these behaviorists are right about their theories of mis-pricing about the market, it should create money-making opportunities for either them or their clients. They should be able to start mutual funds that make trades based on their theories of the market's mis-pricing, buying underpriced assets and selling overpriced ones. If they are right about their behaviorist theories, their mutual funds should be exceptionally good long-term performers, dramatically outperforming the market indexes. Unfortunately, no such mutual fund exists in real life. A study of all existing mutual funds shows none that have outperformed the market consistently, and that in total they all underperform by an amount just about equal to the fees they charge for their advice. Now, you see what economists mean by no free lunch, not even a morsel. If the behaviorists know something with regard to market inefficiency, to date they have not acted on that knowledge in the markets.

So, what am I doing writing this book? Market theory predicts that the current high home prices are a good predictor of future home price performance, and we know that real markets are less susceptible to bubbles and crashes because of efficient pricing, and that because some participants are irrational does not make the entire market pricing system irrational or inefficient. But I hold the opposite view. I believe that current home prices are artificially high and due for a major correction downward. And I don't think the reason is because the market participants are irrational. As a matter of fact I believe that the homeowners and lenders and guarantors are doing exactly what you or I would do in a similar situation—namely, they are each acting very rationally. So how can I conclude that the market is overvalued? The answer is that the housing market in the United States is not a true "market" at all.

The Housing Sector Is Not a True Economic Market

Economists mean something very specific when they talk about "free markets," and there are a number of very important underlying assumptions that must be met before transactions or exchanges can be characterized as belonging to a market, with its guarantees of efficiency and rational pricing.

We all remember from Economics 101 that the exchanges in a free market must be first of all voluntary and noncoercive. In the case of our housing market this appears to be satisfied as no one is forcing us to take out a mortgage or buy a house (spouses don't count). Second, the exchanges must be at arm's length. We will reexamine this assumption when we talk about real estate appraisers and their close incestual relationship to mortgage bankers later in this chapter. Third, the benefits and costs of the transaction must accrue fully to the price negotiators. To the extent that there are costs that might fall upon third parties not represented during the negotiated pricing, such as U.S. taxpayers if the U.S. government is providing debt guarantees, we may have a serious problem with the pricing mechanism for homes and mortgages.

Finally, and most important for my argument that homes are overpriced in today's market, is the requirement that a market have many willing participants, that is, numerous buyers and sellers. Although there are a large number of willing buyers and sellers in the housing marketplace in the form of homeowners, it is my contention that their actions are controlled by a very few number of very large lending institutions. In a world where most of the buyers are leveraged over 80 percent with mortgage debt, I argue that the mortgage lender and his lending terms are the key ingredients to setting home prices in America. We will see that because of competition between these very few lenders, they end up with very aggressive lending policies, which drive up housing prices with little real recourse to the lending institutions. Finally, we will explore the impact that an implied government guarantee has on the operations of Fannie Mae and Freddie Mac, those unfortunate private companies that must compete with them, and the overall mortgage and housing industries.

If indeed the housing market is not a real economic market, this has very serious ramifications. Most important, participants cannot assume that prices are rational. They cannot assume that bubbles will not occur. In a market system, individual participants need not do a lot of investigatory work with regard to the reasonableness of prices because they know it is a market and by definition the prices have to be reasonable. Going back to the racetrack analogy, the guy picking horses based on the color of the silks has just as good a chance of winning as the Ph.D. in statistics sitting next to him. The reason is that the final odds, or the price of each horse's chances of winning, reflect all available information, even all of the Ph.D.'s hard statistical work. The railbird is able to get a "free ride" on the hard statistical work of others and is given the same odds or pricing as the Ph.D. for every horse in the race.

But if the housing market is not a pure market, are homebuyers making a mistake when they assume that the price they are paying is a market price so it must, de facto, be fair? Most of their investigative work before buying is to determine the market price of other homes in the neighborhood, but if this is not a true market what good is this "market" information? This should scare most homebuyers as almost all information they have about a home's value comes from appraisals based completely on the prices of similar properties sold recently in the "market."

Will Interest Rates Stay Low Forever?

One of the primary mistakes that lenders are making in this environment is that they are acting as if the current low interest rate environment will go on forever. MBAs are taught in business school that today's interest rates are the best predictors of future rates, but this does not mean that today's interest rate must be tomorrow's rate with certainty. This does not mean that you should not have contingency plans for different rate environments in the future.

Similarly, people extending trillions of dollars of mortgage credit should allow that interest rates in the future will be anything but exactly equal to the current level. Now, homeowners try to manage this interest rate risk when they lock in rates for 30 years, and banks try to do

this when they try to match the maturities of their assets and their liabilities, but they do a poor job of it when it comes time to determining
the amount of money to lend to any particular homeowner. I have yet
to meet the homeowner who spends less on a house than he or she qualifies for, so it is this qualifying formula which is the prime driver of
how high housing prices will go. It is a big problem because all lenders
use a very similar formula and there are not that many lenders in the
marketplace.

Very simply, when mortgage interest rates drop from 8 to 6 percent,
the qualifying formula says that a family, whose income has not changed,
can now afford a house with a 25 percent higher price. As with any good
self-fulfilling prophecy, housing prices immediately increase 25 percent.
The homeowner sees no benefit to the rate cut as his lower interest costs
are eaten up by the higher home costs. But the world is substantially different in one major regard. Interest rates are lower, but there is no guarantee they will remain low forever.

What if interest rates return to 8 percent sometime in the future? The
existing homeowners initially appear not to be affected as they have
hopefully locked in their 6 percent financing costs for 30 years. The
banks are not initially affected because they have resold their 6 percent
mortgages to Fannie Mae and Freddie Mac. Even these large quasi-gov-
ernment institutions feel rather invulnerable because they have borrowed
in the market at low rates or packaged the mortgages into pass-through
securities and sold them to investors.

But the market is definitely affected. Prices will definitely come
down as banks readjust their qualifying formulas for new homebuyers.
New homebuyers will qualify for 25 percent less financing and this will
have a direct impact on the prices of homes in the future.

So why should the typical homeowner care if housing prices decline?
The answer is that if they are leveraged with 80 percent mortgage debt
and prices decline 25 percent, they will find their housing investment is
underwater. No, their basement will still be dry, but the value of their
home will be less than the amount of debt that they owe on it. We will
see in Chapter 8 that this is not a good state of affairs for an individual
family, and definitely not a good state for the economy. The ability to
sell homes is greatly reduced, thus causing a decline in labor mobility

as people have difficulty accepting new better-paying jobs out of town, thereby creating a drag on the general economy.

So here we have an example of a situation in which both the home-owner and the lender may be acting perfectly rationally, but the ensuing result is less than optimal. First, the small number of lending institutions creates an unhealthy environment where they all coalesce with the same qualifying formula. Second, asking individual homeowners or lenders to properly evaluate such a systemic risk that affects the overall econ-omy so broadly is unfair and probably also outside the scope of most economics textbooks. It is precisely this type of externality that free mar-kets have the greatest degree of trouble with and the reason that all mar-kets must be regulated to assure that they are acting in the general public interest. While most economists are rightly complaining about too much unnecessary regulation, far fewer appreciate the necessary regulations required for the proper functioning of a market system. There is nothing about a market system that says that the resulting transactions will be good for society in general, only that the participants should be better off from their exchanges.

We shall see that in addition to an interest rate increase, home prices would also be negatively affected by a general slowing of the economy, with a commensurate decline in interest rates. Regardless of the direc-tion interest rates head, the end result on housing prices is the same—negative!

What's Wrong with Leverage?

As we saw in Chapter 3, many homeowners are very highly leveraged. Many have purchased homes in the last three years with maximum amounts of debt, and many have refinanced their homes as rates have declined. Unfortunately, many of these refinancings involved releverag-ing the property back up to 80 or 90 percent loan-to-value ratios. In addi-tion to paying off the old high-cost mortgage, many who refinanced took it as an opportunity to repay credit card balances, student loans, auto and boat loans, or to make general improvements on their home. If there was borrowing capacity left over, homeowners ended up buying bigger cars and faster boats. Besides the high amount of debt on their homes, there are a couple of additional problems with these transactions.

First, encouraged by tax laws that make mortgage interest deductible, the homeowner was motivated to consolidate his unsecured debts and give up a security interest in his home to his previously unsecured creditors. Now, if he has trouble paying what was his credit card balance, his home is at risk.

Second, in Hollywood there is an expression that the budget for a picture is "up on the screen." What they mean is that all the moneys contributed to the making of the movie went into direct costs for the picture—actors, director, script, producer, costumes, scenery, etc. There was no leakage of funds to other non–picture-related ventures. This is important because a lender to the picture wants to know that his asset, the picture, is composed of all the budget moneys spent to date. It is his only assurance that moneys contributed actually went to improving the quality of the asset. This is important in any secured-type lending because if there is a problem, selling the asset is the only recourse a creditor has in trying to recoup his investment.

With home refinancings, there is no such guarantee. Lenders can extend moneys, and debt can be attached to the property, but the funds can be appropriated for numerous and varied purposes other than improving the quality of the home. When one borrows against his or her home and uses the money to buy a car or repay credit card debt, the money is definitely not "up on the screen." The housing asset's quality has not improved, but the debt attached to the property has grown dramatically. In any secured lending business, this is a recipe for disaster.

The dramatic amount of leverage utilized by the homebuyer also can contribute to a scenario in which home prices are overvalued. Because home purchasers are often required to only put 1 to 10 percent of the total purchase price down in cash, they in effect are playing with other people's money. Milton Friedman has posited that we manage our own money best and that if we are asked to buy something with other people's money the ensuing mess is only surpassed by a situation in which we are asked to buy something for someone else with someone else's money.

Certainly, there is legal recourse if we fail to repay mortgage moneys, but under Chapter 13 of the Bankrupcy Code we can miss payments and still not subject our house to foreclosure. Call it irrational, but we are much more likely to pay big mortgage banker fees if they tack it onto the debt balance than if we have to pay them in cash up front. Similarly, we would be more likely to pay a higher price for a home if the banker is willing to finance it. We make our investment decisions relative to a home budget, and if a new home appears with project financing attached that does not disturb that budget, we will be much more likely to act. In addition, we can take a false sense of confidence from the fact that the banker is willing to extend the credit. Our thinking goes, well the house doesn't look worth it, and I know I'm not this good of a credit risk, but if this knowledgeable mortgage banker says so, it must be and I must be.

Once a homeowner leaps in logic to realizing he is playing with other people's money, his entire motivation changes. Now he can think of himself as an option holder—where for a small amount of money he can control the upside of a very large and expensive piece of real estate. If worse comes to worse, he can always walk away, leaving the property to the bank and work his way through the bankruptcy court. This is a very rational approach to wealth maximization. If the average American has a net worth of $70,000, mostly in his home, and banks are willing to lend him $300,000 to buy a beautiful new home, his downside is the $15,000 required down payment plus as much of the $55,000 of his remaining net worth the bank can get their hands on. The upside is a home that might double in value every five years, if historical trends hold. Option theory says that such an individual, far from avoiding risk, will seek out highly volatile pricing situations that maximize the value of his option. More importantly, if given the chance to own a small home or a large expensive home, such an option investor will always choose the biggest property with the most leverage. So much for the concept of the homeowner controlling his pricing behavior. And yet no economist would accuse him of acting irrationally. Looking at the home purchase as an option contract means that the homeowner is encouraged to take greater risks, buy bigger properties, and utilize the maximum amount of leverage.

Do Banks and Appraisers Act Rationally?

Surely, large commercial banks will be motivated to act rationally in this process. Surely, if the banks make stupid loans, these loans will eventually come back to haunt them in higher default rates, lower corporate earnings, reduced share prices, lowered debt ratings, and higher long-term borrowing costs—at least that is what my economics textbook says.

Unfortunately, we have seen time and time again that the internal organizations of very large financial institutions are not necessarily geared to reflect market and economic reality. First, individuals at the bank make lending decisions, and not the corporate institution itself. Business organizations try very hard to align the interests of their individual employees with the corporation's goals and objectives, but in a very large institution this is incredibly difficult, if not impossible. Individuals can be motivated by hefty bonuses to bring in mortgage loan business and maximize fee income, but it is very difficult to punish them for defaults, especially if they occur much later after the loans were booked, or occur all at the same time due to some systemic problems in the system. Thus employees also act like option holders in that they are much more concerned with the potential upside of a transaction than its downside. I mean, you can only get fired once, but the upside of success is limitless. I have never known of a company employee who had to pay his company if he erred and the firm lost money. To the extent that managers of the bank are indeed real common stock option holders in their company only exacerbates this option upside and couples it with a limited downside mentality.

The large fees attached to mortgage loans and the attractive profit spreads between the mortgage yields and the banks' cost of funds means that the banks and their employees will be very motivated to add mortgage loans aggressively to their portfolio. Well maybe not make them a permanent addition to their portfolio, but to book them aggressively.

There is a second fundamental economic problem in industries, such as mortgage banking, insurance, or airlines that deal with long-term assets and liabilities. Because traumatic-type events only occur once in a great while, the managers are motivated to offer noneconomic terms in order to generate business. This leads to tougher and tougher price competition followed by very regular industry shakeouts. In the mortgage business this means you have to offer incredibly aggressive terms with regard to total amounts of lending, rates, degree of leverage allowed, etc., or your competitor will, and you will lose a customer. This almost ensures that home prices will be overinflated eventually

Banks have another important reason not to worry a great deal about the credit quality of their mortgage lending—75 percent of the mortgage loans they originate get sold and never appear on their balance sheet. Most are sold to Fannie Mae or Freddie Mac. We will see in Chapter 9 what risks these very large entities introduce into the system. But for now, they act as buyers of mortgages, such that the bank never has to feel any pain if transactions were done at too high a price or with too much debt and end up in default or foreclosure. With this as the end game, there is no reason for the bank to worry about what price homes achieve—it is not going to be their worry. We will see in the end who ought to worry. (Look to your left, look to your right, all three of you may turn out to be suckers.)

Another reason to be concerned about a possible housing crash has to do with how appraisals in the housing industry are done. Typically, when you do an appraisal of an asset or business you look at what the asset's value might be under many different markets or scenarios. For example, if you are appraising a small business, you would want to know what its market value had been historically, what it might garner if sold today in the merger market, the price you could get if you took it public in the stock market, the proceeds realized if you had to quickly liquidate it and sell its hard property and equipment in the real estate and real property markets, and even what price the management could pay if they borrowed and bought the business as a leveraged buyout.

It turns out that home real estate appraisals are much less thorough. It is the nature of most home properties that they aren't really good for much other than as a home. That means that their sole value is in the housing market. It is hard to imagine selling a home in order that it be converted to a church, school, or office.

As we have seen, given the dramatic increase in the price of homes, appraisers put little weight on historical pricing. All they care about is indicators of current market pricing—the best indicator of which is what other similar homes have sold for recently in the neighborhood. To the extent that other recent sales might be overpriced due to some of the systemic problems raised here, this assures that the appraisal will be overpriced. As if this were not enough of a self-fulfilling feedback loop, Fannie Mae increases the maximum amount that they will lend in a conventional mortgage each year by indexing it to, you guessed it, an index of home prices. As home prices increase, Fannie Mae is authorized to lend more in each conventional mortgage, and as Fannie Mae lends more, housing prices increase. Which do you think comes first, the chicken or the egg? Everything in the system, pricing, financing, buyouts, and appraisals are all tied together and racing forward in a fast and furious dance. Where will you be when the clock at the ball strikes 12 and where will your dance partners be?

The problem is worsened, if that could be possible, by questionable practices on behalf of mortgage brokers and appraisers. It is common knowledge that the first piece of news an appraiser hears after getting a new business call from a mortgage banker is the dollar amount of the appraisal necessary to justify the amount of borrowing the homeowner needs to do. If you want to borrow $240,000 you better have a $300,000 house, and I know just the appraiser to make sure that you do. It reminds me of the story of the guy who said his dog was worth $10,000. When challenged by his friend on how he was so sure he had a $10,000 dog, the dog owner replied, "Well, he better be. I just traded two $5000 cats for him."

Conclusion

So what is this rational argument that home prices are due for a major crash in the very near future? First of all, I don't pretend to be able to foretell the future, so I cannot predict exactly which quarter the crash is likely to occur. I can say that the longer it is delayed, and the higher we allow prices to go, the more severe it will be. The problem is that prices are abnormally high. The fact that they will adjust downward in a crash is the solution, not the problem. The reason we call it a crash is that even if it is as small as a 10 to 20 percent adjustment downward, due to the leverage of individual homeowners, this is sufficient to cause major problems for a great number of families. A move of this magnitude could wipe out the entire equity that many families have in their homes, force some into foreclosure, possibly threaten many families' entire net worth, and act as a detriment to the health of the general economy, as many people will be prevented from selling their homes if the debt balances exceed the market value of their homes.

In the end, what is it that gives us the greatest cause for concern when we look at the precarious heights that home prices have attained? Is it the somewhat crazy irrational behavior of buyers caught up in feeding frenzy? Is it the fact that the housing market, on close inspection, doesn't look like a free market at all? Is it that buyers and lenders are acting more like option holders than prudent property investors and creditors? Is it that the assets are being passed around so fast that it is hard to find the institution ultimately responsible? Or is it simply that a government guarantee has assured irrationality as participants take on greater and greater risk for less and less real profit.

It is all these things. And one more: Through the mechanizations of the modern sophisticated mortgage market, not only has liquidity increased dramatically, all sense of self-policing has disappeared. By dramatically increasing the diversification of holders of mortgage securities, and by getting an implied guarantee from the federal government, arrangers have distilled the impact of defaults to the point that no one seems concerned or involved. As I have seen in my work with poor developing countries that lack democracy, such a lack of a self-policing mechanism is a recipe for disaster. The free markets operate efficiently because smart investors win and bad investors lose. The housing market has been built where everyone seems to win, something that Adam Smith will not allow to continue forever.

Summary of Chapter 4

- A market can be rational even if many of its participants are irrational.
- Real markets should have built-in protection against bubbles and crashes.

- How then can we claim that the housing market is a bubble, ready for a crash, with prices that look irrationally high? We claim the housing market is not a real economic market.
- A few lenders in the housing market control the majority of the capital and their very similar qualifying formulas determine prices homeowners will pay for their houses.
- Current low rates will not stay low forever. If they increase in the future, housing prices will contract, as new buyers will qualify for much less funding.
- Recent refinancings have added additional leverage and risk to the system.
- Highly leveraged homeowners are playing with other people's money and therefore are willing to take "option-like" risks.
- Banks are not motivated to control risk in their mortgage lending as they get paid very large fees for these types of transactions, have principal-agent problems with their own employees, and do not hold many of the mortgages on their books, but rather pass them through to quasi agencies and long-term investors.
- Appraisals in the housing industry are suspect because they look only at very recent and local market transactions and appear not to be totally independent judgments of inherent value.
- Self-policing of risk in the mortgage business has all but disappeared.

5

A False Sense of Security

Can Trees Grow to the Sky?

Many homeowners that we speak to are comforted by the fact that home prices have not only increased eightfold over the last 34 years, but have never declined in any single year. Such a record would be admirable for any asset class, especially more recently during a period of lower general inflation. It is relatively easy to exhibit consistent growth during inflationary periods, when everything is increasing in price due to expansive monetary policy, but quite rare when an asset class shows real growth every year during periods of low inflation. To have such real increases in prices signifies that people are valuing the benefits they get from their homes more each year relative to their other purchases.

U.S. housing prices have increased 39 percent during the last five years. General price inflation during this time period has only been 12 percent. This means that, on average, all the homes in America have experienced a real price increase of approximately 27 percent during these five years. We will see in the next chapter that some areas of the country had greater price appreciation than others, but as an average figure for all homes this is a rather remarkable statistic. Empiricists who put great currency in historical experience will see this ever-increasing trend line as the perfect reason to forecast its rising trajectory far into the future. We all have met people who, when challenged about the price paid on their recent home purchase, say that they are extremely confident about the investment because they, their parents, and their friends have never lost money in the housing market.

A theorist might come to the opposite conclusion. He might reason that if homes were properly valued five years ago, and there is no reason to think that they were not, then an asset that has grown 27 percent in real terms over five years might be significantly overvalued today. He would argue that there has not been any dramatic change in people's desire for nice housing, especially over such a short time period as five years. Ed Leamer of UCLA says it best when he meets people that say the reason that home prices are escalating on the California coast is because there is only so much fixed supply of beachfront property available before you run out of coastline. Ed's argument to them is, "What's changed? Wasn't there the same amount of coastline five years ago? If the scarcity value were priced into the beachfront property today, wouldn't it have been priced into the property five years ago?" Beachfront property probably should cost more than property located inland, but that does not mean that it should be growing faster in price over time.

As recently as three years ago, we heard people talk like this—about the potential for trees to grow to the sky—only they were talking about the stock market in the late 1990s. At the time we forgave their naivety because many of them were younger than 40 and had never lived through a major market crash. We allowed them the mistakes all rookie investors make when assuming that companies achieving record earnings deserve record P/E multiples, or that every company that showed two good years of earnings growth was certain to become the next Microsoft. If you apply a record-high P/E to record levels of earnings, it is a potential problem. P/Es are typically very big when companies are just starting to grow and have very low current earnings, but great growth potential. Big P/Es applied to cyclical high earnings never make sense.

At its peak, the Internet stock boom had Internet companies valued at P/Es that suggested growth rates such that there would be more aggregate virtual Internet stock value in the country than traditional bricks-and-mortar business value within only five years. Virtual companies with 500 employees were valued higher in aggregate in the market than old-line companies with 250,000 workers.

It is quite amazing that this occurred in the largest and most sophisticated market in the world. It is even more amazing that these same people seem to be making the same mistakes with their home investments today. Propelled by loose credit and the belief that there will always be a greater fool to pay an even higher price in the future, homebuyers seem to have placed no limit on the prices they will pay.

Homeowners Have Been Lulled to Sleep

In addition to the upward historical trend in home prices, there are a number of other issues that have contributed to a false sense of security in the housing market. The major rationalization most homeowners give when asked if they worry about the high level of home prices is, "You have to live somewhere." The thinking goes that as long as you own just one house, and not multiple houses, that if your home goes down in price, so likely, will all the other homes in the neighborhood. You will be poorer on paper, but not relative to other homeowners. In other words, they believe that a housing price decline will not limit their ability to sell their home, at a lower price, and move to a comparable property, again at a lower price.

There are two problems with this logic. First, in the next chapter we will see that in some cities homes are much higher priced than in others. If you live in one of these cities, and a housing crash comes, your home may fall more than the national average. You may lose your entire home equity and thus preclude your ability to easily move to a different city.

Second, even if homes in all the cities fell by exactly the same amount, leveraged homeowners might find themselves in an impossible situation. Their job may require them to relocate, but because their home value will be less than their mortgage value, they will be stuck. If they lost their job or had a different type of financial crisis, they might be forced to sell into a down market, lose their entire home equity, or worse, possibly have to claim personal bankruptcy and lose their home to foreclosure.

Many homeowners gain comfort about their mortgage debt levels by noticing that, if needed, they could always rent their home, and the rent would cover the mortgage payments. The fallacy in this thinking is that if the economy deteriorates, due to war, deficits, reduced consumer borrowing and spending, or lack of labor mobility because of underwater home mortgages, there is no guarantee that rents will stay at levels sufficiently high to fund mortgage debt. As Ed Leamer has shown in the San Francisco market, rents and apartment building prices have already begun to head down with absolutely no impact on housing prices. If Ed is right, and I think he is, you cannot have a disconnect between the rental market and the home property market for long without lower rents dragging home prices down eventually. Just as the astronomical P/Es of the Internet stocks had to come back to earth, so too housing market P/Es, or housing prices divided by rents, have to remain reasonable. A true value bubble occurs when housing prices increase with no corresponding increase in housing rents.

It is somewhat ironic, but homeowners are also taking great comfort in the current low interest rate environment. Such low rates are pushing homebuyers to pay a great deal more for housing than they would ever have predicted. The greatest mistake lenders and homeowners make in determining prices to pay for housing and the level of debt to take on is the assumption that current interest rates will be stable forever. The homeowner does his part to limit his exposure if he locks in interest rates by entering into a 30-year fixed rate mortgage contract. What he fails to account for is that if rates increase, the next buyer will qualify for much less financing and therefore be able to offer much less in the way of a price.

I love examples like this in economics, where the person who suffers in the long term is the one who only thinks of problems from his own narrow self-interest and is incapable of putting himself in the shoes of someone else—here, another future potential homebuyer. If someone has to suffer economically, why not let it be the self-centered person who has the most difficulty seeing things from other people's perspectives?

We have not spoken about borrowers with adjustable rate mortgages (ARMs). While the percentage of people utilizing ARMs has declined from approximately 30 to 10 percent, there are recent reports that this percentage may have reversed and may be headed back up to 20 percent. Later in the book, we shall see that ARM borrowers will play a very serious role in the increasing interest rate scenario that I lay out in Chapter 8. Here, let me say that their false security must be twofold. One, they must have some strong misplaced belief that interest rates will stay low forever. Two, they must have taken great comfort in the fact that their mortgages have rate limits as to the amount that they can adjust upward each year if rates head back up. When mortgage rates were 15 percent, a 3 percent cap on rate increases for ARM borrowers each year must have provided real comfort. But today, with ARM rates of 4 percent, a 3 percent increase could nearly double the homeowner's monthly payments, and that would only be a 12-month limit. ARM borrowers might find themselves out on the street and living under the bridge before their final rate caps are enacted.

Finally, homeowners have grown accustomed to a world of aggressive mortgage brokers, realtors, and bankers. It is hard to imagine a future world in which "For Sale" signs stand on lawns for years rather than days, where instead of multiple offers above the asking price, you are faced with taking numerous discounts to your asking price, where you need to serve lunch at your open house just to get the brokers to come over and look, and where banks have retrenched with new lending policies that include asking questions like what did this property sell for 10 years ago. If bankers retrench, and we assure you that is what they do for a living (just ask any farmer in the Midwest), then all the formulas you know for lending and pricing go out the window. There will be no comparables in the neighborhood because nothing will be selling. Bankers will have to go back to very realistic valuations, probably based on square footage and historical pricing. Valuations will further be damaged by the banks' own activity as they dump foreclosed properties on the market at huge discounts to the mortgage amount. Banks really do not want to hold bad loans on their books, because it only reminds them of managerial errors of the past. They are infamous for buying high and selling low when it comes to foreclosures. Unfortunately, their aggressive selling will only exacerbate an already weak property market.

To homeowners this means that whatever rosy assumptions they had about refinancing, taking money out in the form of a second mortgage equity loan, or selling at a high price to a buyer financed by aggressive bank formulas will all basically evaporate at the same time. When an entire market's sense of value is based solely on current "market" values, then be prepared for a wild ride when those market prices come under attack from a less aggressive banking sector.

Bankers and Regulators Have Also Been Lulled to Sleep

It is not only the homeowner who has been comforted by a constantly increasing market for home prices. The supposed experts—realtors, appraisers, mortgage bankers, commercial bankers, and even Fannie Mae and Freddie Mac—are all showing signs of dozing off. It is true that lending institutions and mortgage investors take great care to limit their exposure to interest rate and early principal repayment risks in their portfolios. There is much less they can do to limit their exposure to default risk in their mortgage portfolio.

The two traditional methods for limiting exposure to default risk in a housing mortgage portfolio are to limit the amount of each loan relative to the property's market value and to diversify geographically. Because of competitive pressures it is very difficult to run a conservative bank in the mortgage lending business and only work with big down-payment customers. If you don't do a no-points, low-fee, 97 percent loan-to-value mortgage, the guy down the street certainly will.

As far as diversifying geographically, this has been an excellent strategy to date because most of our country's housing problems historically have had an epicenter to them: the Internet bust hit Seattle and San Jose, the oil glut hit Houston and Dallas, and Wall Street's corruption scandal will most likely hit New York worst of all. But what if the next problem were national in scope? The two biggest problems I am forecasting here are exactly that: interest rates increasing nationally and overly aggressive lending formulas being applied across all areas of the country. To the extent that there is a systemic problem with the way the entire mortgage industry extends credit, then geographic diversification is much less effective in stemming default losses.

We shall see in Chapter 9 that even the AAA-rated behemoths of the mortgage business, Fannie Mae and Freddie Mac, are not without risk. We shall see that they have added incredible amounts of leverage to their businesses. How they got their triple-A rating might have more to do with the financial health of the U.S. taxpayer than with either institution's credit analysis, as they lean heavily on their implied government guarantee. Many of their most highly leveraged mortgages depend on private mortgage insurance (PMI) providers for risk management, and these providers themselves are beginning to feel a bit of a pinch. It would only seem prudent to ask the question: what would have to happen before these PMI providers themselves were at risk?

Again, Fannie Mae and Freddie Mac have gained comfort by utilizing the most sophisticated forms of interest rate hedging and maturity matching. But, given the degree of leveraging throughout the system, they have probably not done as adequate a job as they should in analyzing how they would fare in a real housing price downturn with a significant number of foreclosures.

What about the government's supervision and regulation of Fannie Mae and Freddie Mac? Shouldn't you gain some comfort knowing that the largest lending operations in the world are well supervised? Well, to start, they are exempt from SEC filing requirements and from any supervision by the SEC. They therefore are not subject to filing accounting statements with the SEC. Their financial statements are enormously convoluted, and given the large amount of derivatives and hedging business that they do, it is next to impossible to figure out how their basic mortgage operations are doing.

Fannie Mae shows earnings of some $15 billion in pretax cash flow each year, and yet it only trades at a total market capitalization of $60 billion. Such a four-times-free cash flow multiple is typical of a zero-growth company, not one of the only two companies in the S&P 500 that has shown double-digit growth in revenues and earnings for each of the last 20 years. It seems that others in the marketplace are as confused as the author is about how their accounting works.

Next, we challenge anyone to name the government agency that has the responsibility of supervising these monoliths. Give up? It is the Office of Federal Housing Enterprise Oversight. Never heard of it? Join the club. I worked for 12 years on Wall Street and until I sat down to write this book I had never heard of it either. Well, how tough of a regulator is this outfit? Who knows? I've never heard of a single regulation that they have passed that forced compliance on Fannie Mae or Freddie Mac, nor have I heard of one violation they have made public. The reason is probably very simple. Fannie Mae and Freddie Mac are two of the biggest financial contributors to Congress. The only thing better than being subject to lax SEC regulation is to have your own regulator under the direct control of a well-paid Congress.

We have seen that many of the participants in the housing industry, mistakenly, have been lulled into a false sense of security. Chapter 6 addresses the question of regional versus national economies in the home real estate market.

Summary of Chapter 5

- The fact that housing seems to have increased in value every single year has given homeowners a false sense of security that what went up cannot come down.
- Many homeowners mistakenly perceive no risk in housing because they only own one home and they have to live somewhere.
- Homeowners think they will always be able to rent their home at today's rent levels if they have a problem in the future.
- Homeowners have not thought through the ramifications of a world with higher interest rates.
- Borrowers with adjustable rate mortgages must believe either that the current low interest rates are here permanently or that their interest rate caps will protect them from higher rates.

- Banks and mortgage lenders think geographic diversification will protect them in a downturn. They don't realize that the next downturn in housing prices could be a national event.
- Mortgage lenders think they are adequately hedged against interest rate risk. They have done a poor job of protecting themselves against potentially significant default risk.

Are High Home Prices a Regional or National Problem?

Housing Prices in Metropolitan Areas

Although this book has identified a number of problems in the housing market that are national in scope, we would be remiss not to look at the major metropolitan areas of our country to see how each is fairing with regard to housing prices. Although they all would suffer if rates increased or banks retrenched in their lending terms, it only seems logical that those regional markets that have appreciated the most might have the most to lose in a downturn. Again, we will face the question of relative value.

The first approach in identifying metropolitan areas most at risk to a price decline in residential real estate is to ask which areas had the greatest price appreciation over the last five years. Table 6.1 shows those metropolitan areas that had the greatest price appreciation over the past five years, each city on the list having a cumulative appreciation of at least 35 percent.

TABLE 6.1 The 40 Fastest Growing Housing Markets

Ranking by Growth Rate	Metropolitan Area*	5-Year Growth Rate in Housing Prices
1	San Francisco Bay Area, CA	78.4%
2	San Diego, CA	74.9%
3	Boston, MA	73.0%
4	Nassau/Suffolk, NY	72.0%
5	Orange Cnty. (Anaheim/Santa Ana MSA), CA	64.1%
6	Minneapolis/St. Paul, MN/WI	60.3%
7	Denver, CO	60.1%
8	New York/N. New Jersey/Long Island, NY/NJ/CT	60.0%
9	Sacramento, CA	59.7%
10	Charleston, SC	56.5%
11	Monmouth/Ocean, NJ	56.3%
12	Los Angeles Area, CA	55.2%
13	Bergen/Passaic, NJ	52.7%
14	Portland, ME	52.7%
15	Providence, RI	52.2%
16	Riverside/San Bernardino, CA	51.9%
17	Newark, NJ	51.0%
18	Ft. Lauderdale/Hollywood/Pompano Beach, FL	50.1%
19	Atlantic City, NJ	49.0%
20	Tampa/St. Petersburg/Clearwater, FL	48.0%
21	Middlesex/Somerset/Hunterdon, NJ	47.9%
22	Sarasota, FL	47.6%
23	Seattle, WA	47.3%
24	Ft. Myers/Cape Coral, FL	46.3%
25	Washington, DC/MD/VA	45.9%
26	Jacksonville, FL	45.0%
27	Trenton, NJ	44.7%
28	Austin/San Marcos, TX	44.6%
29	Miami/Hialeah, FL	44.1%
30	New Haven/Meriden, CT	43.2%
31	Orlando, FL	40.2%
32	Daytona Beach, FL	40.2%
33	Atlanta, GA	40.0%
34	Phoenix, AZ	38.2%
35	Houston, TX	38.0%
36	Kansas City, MO/KS	36.8%

*All areas are metropolitan statistical areas (MSAs) as defined by the U.S. Office of Management and Budget as of 1992. They include the named central city and surrounding areas.

37	Hartford, CT	36.8%
38	Melbourne/Titusville/Palm Bay, FL	35.8%
39	Baltimore, MD	35.6%
40	Colorado Springs, CO	35.6%

Source: Office of Federal Housing Enterprise Oversight

It is interesting to note that of the more than 200 that reported data, only one city in the country had a decline in its average housing price over the last 12 months ending June 30, 2002, and that was San Jose, California, which saw a decline of 3.7 percent. This is an incredible statistic given how soft the national economy has been recently and gives further testimony to the theory that homes are overvalued relative to all other economic activity.

Any price appreciation over the last five years due to a lower interest rate environment should have been relatively constant across the regions of the country. If you assume that these markets were properly priced five years ago, then barring any new burning desires by people to want to live in these towns with faster-growing home prices, they would be the most suspect to have overinflated home property markets. It could be that the price increases realized were indeed real and deserved in the short run, but over time should return to a more normal level as the high prices will drive some homeowners to less expensive towns, prevent businesses from relocating to the area, and encourage new building by home construction companies.

It also turns out that there is a correlation in that the more expensive cities for housing five years ago showed the greatest growth in prices during the following five years (see Figure 6.1). If you believe that the rich get richer, this may seem intuitive to you. Or if you come from the momentum school of stock investing, you probably recognize this phenomenon. Momentum investing says that the fastest growing in the past will be the fastest growing in the future. But if you believe that all housing is somewhat similar, you would have expected the undervalued, or less expensive cities, to appreciate faster and try to catch up to their wealthier neighbors. Just as our country's citizens are slowly bifurcating into wealthier and poorer, so it seems our nation's cities are splitting into lands of haves and have-nots.

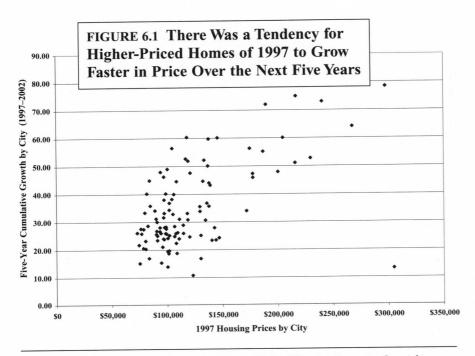

FIGURE 6.1 There Was a Tendency for Higher-Priced Homes of 1997 to Grow Faster in Price Over the Next Five Years

Source: National Association of Realtors and Office of Federal Housing Enterprise Oversight

In addition to growth rates, it probably makes sense to examine absolute levels of housing prices as a predictor of which cities might be most overvalued. Although the highest-priced cities grew the fastest historically, this cannot go on forever.

Table 6.2 shows the 15 most expensive large metropolitan areas in the United States and the 15 least expensive, judged solely by the level of housing prices. A thorough analysis of the relative real estate values in the country, one to determine why a home is worth $530,000 in San Francisco but only $89,600 in El Paso, Texas, would be an economist's nightmare. It would not only involve quantifiable variables like average incomes in the area, job prospects, and regional economic growth prospects, but also more subjective measures like how nice the weather is, what the restaurants are like, is there any culture to speak of, what is the crime rate, how friendly are the natives, and is there a college or pro football team nearby.

TABLE 6.2 The 15 Most and Least Expensive Housing Markets

Ranking by Price	Metropolitan Area*	Housing Price October 2002
	Most Expensive	
1	San Francisco Bay Area, CA	$530,900
2	Orange Cnty. (Anaheim/Santa Ana MSA), CA	$439,400
3	Boston, MA	$415,800
4	San Diego, CA	$379,200
5	Bergen/Passaic, NJ	$351,000
6	Honolulu, HI	$345,000
7	New York/N. New Jersey/Long Island,NY/NJ/CT	$328,000
8	Newark, NJ	$326,200
9	Nassau/Suffolk, NY	$326,200
10	Middlesex/Somerset/Hunterdon, NJ	$296,300
11	Los Angeles Area, CA	$290,000
12	Monmouth/Ocean, NJ	$273,500
13	Seattle, WA	$261,500
14	Washington, DC/MD/VA	$259,300
15	Denver, CO	$233,600
	Least Expensive	
109	Rochester, NY	$97,900
110	Davenport/Moline/Rock Island, IA/IL	$97,200
111	Amarillo, TX	$97,100
112	Corpus Christi, TX	$97,000
113	Little Rock-N. Little Rock, AR	$97,000
114	Oklahoma City, OK	$96,700
115	South Bend/Mishawaka, IN	$94,600
116	Topeka, KS	$93,900
117	Shreveport, LA	$92,400
118	Peoria, IL	$91,900
119	Syracuse, NY	$90,600
120	Waterloo/Cedar Falls, IA	$89,900
121	El Paso, TX	$89,600
122	Beaumont/Port Arthur, TX	$89,200
123	Buffalo/Niagara Falls, NY	$86,600

*All areas are metropolitan statistical areas (MSAs) as defined by the U.S. Office of Management and Budget as of 1992. They include the named central city and surrounding areas.

Source: National Association of Realtors

The wonderful thing about a market-based pricing system is that prices reflect not only all of these factors but many more. It also allows the individual to exercise his free will to choose a location that provides the greatest value to him or her personally. Denver's yearly snowfalls would be torture to an arthritic, but paradise on earth to a powder skier.

Housing Prices as a Multiple of Income in Select Metropolitan Areas

As a first-order approximation of what might be a very important price-determining factor, we looked at the average prices of homes in each of the major metropolitan markets and determined what this average home price was as a multiple of the area's average household income. While obviously ignoring many of the subjective factors discussed above, this will allow us to concentrate on those areas that are probably subject to the most debt leverage relative to household incomes. You may conclude that home prices in San Diego really are worth 6.3 times their average household income based on the beautiful weather, the proximity to the ocean, and the plethora of high-tech and telecommunication jobs nearby. But even if you do make this value judgment, the fact that such a high price is being paid relative to local incomes assures that there will be many cases of extreme debt leverage on homeowners and that it will be a high risk site should prices begin to drop. Remember, 3.0 times income is the maximum recommended level of debt by Ginnie Mae's own affordability formula. And 6.3 is San Diego's multiple based on median home prices and median incomes. Half the homeowners in San Diego paid multiples in excess of 6.3. Just as with the national numbers, we suffer from having to analyze averages of populations. Low incomes of property wealthy retirees, varying ratios of renters versus owners by city, as well as different wealth distributions by city would all lead to bias error in this type of average analysis.

On October 7, 2002, the *Wall Street Journal* reported that cracks are spreading in the foundation of the U.S. housing boom, as evidence mounts that the long run-up in home prices cannot be sustained. In more than 100 U.S. cities, real home prices have climbed twice as fast as household incomes since 1998. In the last two years, real national home prices have tripled the rate of growth of household incomes. On Long Island, housing prices have jumped 81 percent since 1998, while incomes have increased only 14 percent. In Boston, housing is up 89 percent in price since 1998 while incomes have only gained 22 percent. The article quotes Allen Sinai, chief global economist of Decision Economics Inc., "I have never seen an asset market—whether it's stocks or real estate—that has boomed to excessive prices—without a serious downturn. I really doubt we will escape. Asset prices don't go straight up forever."

Figure 6.2 shows a plot of housing prices versus incomes for the major metropolitan areas we studied. While incomes explain 43 percent of the variation in housing prices, you can see by the wide scatter of data points around the linear approximation that there are indeed other factors that influence home value in addition to average household income.

Table 6.3, which provides a summary of housing prices, incomes, and income multiples for our major metropolitan areas, is very illumi-

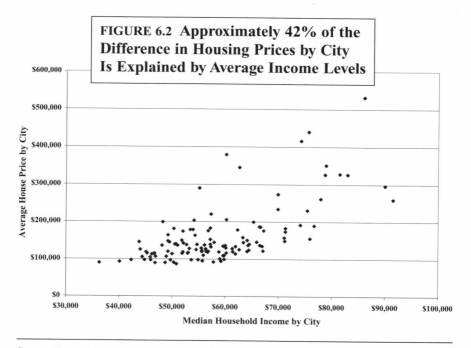

FIGURE 6.2 Approximately 42% of the Difference in Housing Prices by City Is Explained by Average Income Levels

Source: National Association of Realtors for housing prices; Census Bureau for household incomes

nating. The first thing you notice is the striking difference in house prices around the country. Next, you will see that average incomes do not vary nearly as much as house prices, so they cannot fully explain the difference. What results is a calculation of housing income multiples that range from 6.31 times for San Diego to 1.59 times for Peoria, Illinois, and Topeka, Kansas. Eyeballing the list, you will see that the pricier towns tend to be in the Northeast and on the West Coast and seem to have either unusually good weather or be located close to cultural hubs, or both.

TABLE 6.3 Housing Price Analysis by Major Metropolitan Area

Ranking by Multiple	Metropolitan Area*	5 Year Growth Rate in Housing Prices	Housing Price October 2002	Median Household Income	Multiple of Income
1	San Diego, CA	74.9%	$379,200	$60,100	6.31
2	San Francisco Bay Area, CA	78.4%	$530,900	$86,100	6.17
3	Orange Cnty. (Anaheim/Santa Ana MSA), CA	64.1%	$439,400	$75,600	5.81
4	Boston, MA	73.0%	$415,800	$74,200	5.60
5	Honolulu, HI	13.2%	$345,000	$62,600	5.51
6	Los Angeles Area, CA	55.2%	$290,000	$55,100	5.26
7	Bergen/Passaic, NJ	52.7%	$351,000	$78,900	4.45
8	Newark, NJ	51.0%	$326,200	$78,700	4.14
9	Miami/Hialeah, FL	44.1%	$198,800	$48,200	4.12
10	New York/N. New Jersey/Long Island, NY/NJ/CT	60.0%	$328,000	$81,500	4.02
11	Nassau/Suffolk, NY	72.0%	$273,500	$69,900	3.93
12	Monmouth/Ocean, NJ	56.3%	$326,200	$83,000	3.91
13	Sacramento, CA	59.7%	$219,800	$57,300	3.84
14	Providence, RI	52.2%	$203,300	$54,100	3.76
15	Riverside/San Bernardino, CA	51.9%	$181,000	$50,300	3.60
16	Ft. Lauderdale/Hollywood/Pompano Beach, FL	50.1%	$205,500	$60,200	3.41
17	Seattle, WA	47.3%	$261,500	$77,900	3.36
18	Sarasota, FL	47.6%	$178,500	$53,400	3.34
19	Denver, CO	60.1%	$233,600	$69,900	3.34
20	Tacoma, WA	33.9%	$173,600	$52,000	3.34
21	Charleston, SC	56.5%	$164,000	$49,200	3.33
22	Eugene/Springfield, OR	N/A	$145,200	$43,800	3.32
23	Portland, ME	52.7%	$178,500	$53,900	3.31
24	Middlesex/Somerset/Hunterdon, NJ	47.9%	$296,300	$90,000	3.29
25	Portland, OR	24.3%	$182,700	$57,200	3.19

*All areas are metropolitan statistical areas (MSAs) as defined by the U.S. Office of Management and Budget as of 1992. They include the named central city and surrounding areas.

N/A = Not Available.

26	Colorado Springs, CO	35.6%	$175,500	$56,800	3.09
27	Chicago, IL	34.0%	$230,200	$75,400	3.05
28	New Haven/Meriden, CT	43.2%	$199,200	$65,300	3.05
29	Las Vegas, NV	25.2%	$163,200	$54,300	3.01
30	Tucson, AZ	28.9%	$147,600	$49,200	3.00
31	Richland/Kennewick/Pasco, WA	N/A	$144,500	$49,500	2.92
32	Atlantic City, NJ	49.0%	$149,700	$51,800	2.89
33	Reno, NV	23.5%	$178,000	$62,300	2.86
34	New Orleans, LA	28.1%	$125,200	$44,000	2.85
35	Washington, DC/MD/VA	45.9%	$259,300	$91,500	2.83
36	Gainesville, FL	N/A	$135,800	$48,100	2.82
37	Baltimore, MD	35.6%	$186,900	$66,400	2.81
38	Hartford, CT	36.8%	$185,900	$66,600	2.79
39	Tampa/St. Petersburg/Clearwater, FL	48.0%	$139,400	$50,500	2.76
40	Springfield, MA	32.8%	$139,700	$50,700	2.76
41	Ft. Myers/Cape Coral, FL	46.3%	$142,100	$52,100	2.73
42	Albuquerque, NM	10.8%	$136,300	$51,000	2.67
43	Salt Lake City/Ogden, UT	16.8%	$152,100	$57,200	2.66
44	Mobile, AL	26.6%	$118,300	$45,100	2.62
45	Birmingham, AL	26.2%	$138,100	$52,700	2.62
46	Milwaukee, WI	30.7%	$175,900	$67,200	2.62
47	Trenton, NJ	44.7%	$191,700	$74,100	2.59
48	Madison, WI	27.9%	$182,700	$71,300	2.56
49	Pensacola, FL	N/A	$115,000	$45,300	2.54
50	Orlando, FL	40.2%	$138,600	$54,700	2.53
51	Phoenix, AZ	38.2%	$144,300	$57,900	2.49
52	Philadelphia, PA/NJ	33.1%	$157,400	$63,300	2.49
53	Minneapolis/St. Paul, MN/WI	60.3%	$189,400	$76,700	2.47
54	El Paso, TX	N/A	$89,600	$36,300	2.47
55	Daytona Beach, FL	40.2%	$114,700	$46,700	2.46
56	Spokane, WA	13.9%	$114,200	$46,600	2.45
57	Greensboro/Winston-Salem/High Point, NC	24.0%	$137,400	$56,100	2.45
58	Baton Rouge, LA	24.0%	$119,900	$49,200	2.44
59	San Antonio, TX	23.4%	$112,500	$46,200	2.44
60	Raleigh/Durham, NC	23.4%	$173,300	$71,300	2.43
61	Tallahassee, FL	N/A	$138,900	$57,200	2.43
62	Greenville/Spartanburg, SC	25.2%	$127,800	$53,200	2.40
63	Biloxi/Gulfport, MS	N/A	$105,200	$44,400	2.37
64	Charlotte/Gastonia/Rock Hill, NC/SC	24.7%	$150,000	$64,100	2.34
65	Albany/Schenectady/Troy, NY	18.8%	$129,100	$55,500	2.33
66	Memphis, TN/AR/MS	22.4%	$132,300	$57,300	2.31
67	Shreveport, LA	N/A	$92,400	$40,100	2.30
68	Corpus Christi, TX	N/A	$97,000	$42,300	2.29
69	Boise City, ID	24.2%	$124,900	$54,500	2.29
70	Columbus, OH	25.9%	$144,400	$63,400	2.28
71	Knoxville, TN	30.0%	$118,300	$52,000	2.28
72	Charleston, WV	N/A	$104,300	$45,900	2.27
73	Tulsa, OK	33.3%	$106,500	$46,900	2.27
74	Chattanooga, TN/GA	25.6%	$113,500	$50,000	2.27
75	Cleveland, OH	25.9%	$135,800	$60,000	2.26
76	Lexington/Fayette, KY	28.2%	$126,900	$56,300	2.25

77	Houston, TX	38.0%	$134,300	$59,600	2.25
78	Louisville, KY/IN	27.6%	$126,500	$56,300	2.25
79	Canton, OH	26.7%	$114,900	$51,900	2.21
80	Austin/San Marcos, TX	44.6%	$157,000	$71,100	2.21
81	Richmond/Petersburg, VA	31.1%	$145,500	$65,900	2.21
82	Montgomery, AL	N/A	$116,800	$53,000	2.20
83	Jacksonville, FL	45.0%	$122,100	$55,600	2.20
84	Melbourne/Titusville/Palm Bay, FL	35.8%	$115,300	$52,900	2.18
85	Pittsburgh, PA	28.6%	$106,300	$48,900	2.17
86	Amarillo, TX	N/A	$97,100	$44,800	2.17
87	Kansas City, MO/KS	36.8%	$139,700	$64,500	2.17
88	Lansing/East Lansing, MI	33.1%	$129,700	$60,100	2.16
89	Green Bay, WI	24.9%	$133,300	$61,900	2.15
90	Akron, OH	28.0%	$119,700	$55,600	2.15
91	Cincinnati, OH/KY/IN	28.4%	$137,000	$64,300	2.13
92	Columbia, SC	19.5%	$120,000	$56,400	2.13
93	Gary/Hammond, IN	18.7%	$120,200	$56,800	2.12
94	Oklahoma City, OK	25.8%	$96,700	$46,000	2.10
95	Atlanta, GA	40.0%	$148,500	$71,200	2.09
96	Toledo, OH	31.2%	$118,200	$56,700	2.08
97	Grand Rapids, MI	31.6%	$127,500	$61,300	2.08
98	Dallas, TX	34.4%	$137,000	$66,500	2.06
99	Wilmington, DE/NJ/MD	30.8%	$155,200	$75,900	2.04
100	Sioux Falls, SD	26.0%	$119,000	$58,800	2.02
101	Des Moines, IA	N/A	$134,400	$66,900	2.01
102	Lincoln, NE	25.7%	$125,000	$62,600	2.00
103	Fargo/Moorhead, ND/MN	N/A	$109,700	$55,900	1.96
104	Little Rock-N. Little Rock, AR	20.3%	$97,000	$49,700	1.95
105	Saint Louis, MO/IL	34.1%	$119,400	$61,400	1.94
106	Omaha, NE/IA	25.9%	$124,100	$64,400	1.93
107	Dayton/Springfield, OH	21.1%	$116,000	$60,200	1.93
108	Beaumont/Port Arthur, TX	N/A	$89,200	$46,800	1.91
109	Indianapolis, IN	23.8%	$120,400	$64,100	1.88
110	Waterloo/Cedar Falls, IA	N/A	$89,900	$48,700	1.85
111	Appleton/Oshkosh/Neenah, WI	25.0%	$114,100	$61,900	1.84
112	Champaign/Urbana/Rantoul, IL	N/A	$108,900	$59,600	1.83
113	Rockford, IL	15.3%	$109,200	$59,800	1.83
114	Cedar Rapids, IA	19.6%	$121,800	$67,100	1.82
115	Davenport/Moline/Rock Island, IA/IL	27.6%	$97,200	$53,600	1.81
116	Syracuse, NY	21.7%	$90,600	$50,300	1.80
117	Rochester, NY	17.0%	$97,900	$54,900	1.78
118	Buffalo/Niagara Falls, NY	15.1%	$86,600	$50,800	1.70
119	Wichita, KS	27.4%	$100,400	$59,000	1.70
120	South Bend/Mishawaka, IN	20.6%	$94,600	$55,700	1.70
121	Ft. Wayne, IN	23.2%	$99,100	$59,800	1.66
122	Peoria, IL	26.1%	$91,900	$57,800	1.59
123	Topeka, KS	0.0%	$93,900	$59,200	1.59

Sources: National Association of Realtors for housing prices; Census Bureau for household incomes; Office of Federal Housing Enterprise Oversight for 5-year growth rates.

The lower multiples paid in the Midwest may reflect a more con-servative approach to debt management rather than suggesting that real estate there is any less desirable or attractive. The lower multiples might reflect more prudent and conservative management of debt loads on the family's home in the country's heartland than on the coasts. When I was involved in leveraged buyouts on Wall Street in the go-go 80s, the Mid-west companies were the slowest to embrace the 95 percent debt capital structure prevalent in LBOs, and it was they who had the last laugh when the LBO market crashed. Maybe Midwesterners are all too familiar with family histories of losing farms and businesses to overly aggressive bankers when the bankers had a change of heart and began to retrench. Farmers were told that their farms were worth millions and were encour-aged to borrow to buy expensive new equipment, which was repossessed as soon as the bankers decided that their appraisals needed downward adjustment and the same debt levels now looked too high. This same phenomenon, in which banks determine market and appraised value, inflate it, lend against it, reduce the appraisal, and initiate foreclosure is what will happen in many home real estate markets.

I would focus your attention in Table 6.3 to those areas of the coun-try that have average multiples above 3.0. These are the areas of highest risk should there be a price decline. Not only are these the priciest with the greatest room to fall, but they would also be expected to have the most number of highly indebted homeowners. As the worst cases begin to fail, and the banks foreclose and dump them on the market, all prices suffer.

If you are lucky enough not to live in one of these high-multiple areas, you still need to do some analysis. Rather than depend on the town's average multiple, you should probably calculate your own actual debt multiple. You may be one of the highly levered in a less levered town. Add all your debts, mortgage debt, auto loans, credit card balances, student loans, and the debt equivalent of any required alimony payments (say, eight times your annual alimony payment), and then divide by the pretax household income of all workers in the family who will contribute to servicing the mortgage. If greater than three times your household income, you probably want to pay special attention to the second half of this book in which we examine ways to protect your home, your family, and your net worth should there be a housing crash in the near future.

The three relative valuation approaches in Table 6.3 can be utilized in tandem. It would make sense that those metropolitan areas that score poorly on the five-year growth record, the absolute price level, and the multiple of income methodology might be those areas with highest price vulnerability. We have included the five-year growth rates in Table 6.3 so you can peruse this list at your leisure and do a much more personalized analysis as to where your family stands.

Housing Prices Relative to Apartment Building Prices in Select Metropolitan Areas

Ed Leamer and I are currently writing an academic research paper that compares house prices to apartment building prices in selected cities of our country. Ed has long believed that business people who buy apartment buildings as investments are much more savvy about current economic conditions than your average homeowner, who is primarily interested in shelter. Apartment building owners also have to adjust their price thinking rather quickly if there is a softening of the rental market, or else they will begin to lose money. Homeowners are under no such profit pressure and so may take their time in recognizing a price decline. No reason to list a home in a down market and no reason to quickly reduce the asking price on a previously listed home just to get it to sell quickly.

Table 6.4 shows, for the 57 major metropolitan areas for which data were publicly available, how their current housing prices stack up against their apartment building prices. The housing data had to be transposed to a per-square-foot price using national square foot averages for homes for comparison to the apartment building data, which were calculated by square feet. The apartment pricing data are from 2000, but since rental incomes have softened recently, this probably does not affect the overall conclusions.

TABLE 6.4 Housing Prices Relative to Rental Apartment Prices

Metropolitan Area*	Housing Price	Housing Price/ SqFt†	Apartment Price/SqFt‡	Housing Price per SqFt/ Apartment Price per SqFt
Honolulu, HI	$345,000	$200.58	$92.73	2.16
Orange Cnty. (Anaheim/Santa Ana MSA), CA	$439,400	$255.47	$123.86	2.06
Nassau/Suffolk, NY	$326,200	$189.65	$104.04	1.82
San Diego, CA	$379,200	$220.47	$129.80	1.70
Boston, MA	$415,800	$241.74	$146.28	1.65
Seattle, WA	$261,500	$152.03	$94.17	1.61
Newark, NJ	$326,200	$189.65	$120.74	1.57
Ft. Lauderdale/Hollywood/Pompano Beach, FL	$205,500	$119.48	$76.15	1.57
Milwaukee, WI	$175,900	$102.27	$65.41	1.56
Denver, CO	$233,600	$135.81	$86.97	1.56
Sacramento, CA	$219,800	$127.79	$81.85	1.56
Washington, DC/MD/VA	$259,300	$150.76	$97.75	1.54
Miami/Hialeah, FL	$198,800	$115.58	$75.98	1.52
San Francisco Bay Area, CA	$530,900	$308.66	$204.10	1.51
Portland, OR	$182,700	$106.22	$70.82	1.50
Chicago, IL	$230,200	$133.84	$90.89	1.47
Birmingham, AL	$138,100	$80.29	$54.54	1.47
Las Vegas, NV	$163,200	$94.88	$66.93	1.42
Greensboro/Winston-Salem/High Point, NC	$137,400	$79.88	$56.37	1.42
Baltimore, MD	$186,900	$108.66	$76.97	1.41
Hartford, CT	$185,900	$108.08	$77.02	1.40
Greenville/Spartanburg, SC	$127,800	$74.30	$53.33	1.39
Minneapolis/St. Paul, MN/WI	$189,400	$110.12	$80.02	1.38
Columbus, OH	$144,400	$83.95	$61.16	1.37
Albuquerque, NM	$136,300	$79.24	$58.92	1.34
New Orleans, LA	$125,200	$72.79	$54.20	1.34
Salt Lake City/Ogden, UT	$152,100	$88.43	$66.05	1.34
Tampa/St. Petersburg/Clearwater, FL	$139,400	$81.05	$60.92	1.33
Raleigh/Durham, NC	$173,300	$100.76	$77.23	1.30
Cincinnati, OH/KY/IN	$137,000	$79.65	$61.16	1.30
Riverside/San Bernardino, CA	$181,000	$105.23	$82.49	1.28
Austin/San Marcos, TX	$157,000	$91.28	$73.08	1.25
Kansas City, MO/KS	$139,700	$81.22	$65.55	1.24
Charlotte/Gastonia/Rock Hill, NC/SC	$150,000	$87.21	$70.47	1.24
Los Angeles Area, CA	$290,000	$168.60	$137.10	1.23

*All areas are metropolitan statistical areas (MSAs) as defined by the U.S. Office of Management and Budget as of 1992. They include the named central city and surrounding areas.

†Housing prices per square foot are estimated because no data available on difference in average home's square footage by metropolitan area. This study assumes all homes are national average 1,720 square feet.

‡Housing prices as of 9/30/02 and apartment prices as of 1/1/00 as this is the most current publicly available data.

Jacksonville, FL	$122,100	$70.99	$58.78	1.21
Memphis, TN/AR/MS	$132,300	$76.92	$64.49	1.19
Houston, TX	$134,300	$78.08	$66.60	1.17
Tulsa, OK	$106,500	$61.92	$53.00	1.17
Cleveland, OH	$135,800	$78.95	$69.09	1.14
Orlando, FL	$138,600	$80.58	$70.85	1.14
Phoenix, AZ	$144,300	$83.90	$74.90	1.12
Dallas, TX	$137,000	$79.65	$72.44	1.10
Indianapolis, IN	$120,400	$70.00	$66.48	1.05
Atlanta, GA	$148,500	$86.34	$83.17	1.04
Oklahoma City, OK	$96,700	$56.22	$55.99	1.00
San Antonio, TX	$112,500	$65.41	$65.45	1.00
Saint Louis, MO/IL	$119,400	$69.42	$69.54	1.00
Philadelphia, PA/NJ	$157,400	$91.51	$92.44	0.99
Pittsburgh, PA	$106,300	$61.80	$63.61	0.97
El Paso, TX	$89,600	$52.09	$54.07	0.96

Sources: National Association of Realtors for home prices and www.realestateindex.com for apartment building prices

What the table shows is that typically people pay more for their home on a per-square-foot basis than apartment building buyers. This difference could be explained by frothy overvaluations, but it also could be explained by the greater amount of land associated with a house as opposed to a single apartment. Homeowners also get the tax deductibility of mortgage interest on their primary residence, and as we saw, this could explain as much as 10 to 15 percent of the home's total value.

It is interesting to look across cities in this analysis also. Los Angeles seems to have a much lower ratio than San Diego in this analysis. It is more difficult to explain away this difference and so might very well indicate a San Diego housing market that is hyperventilating.

Summary of Chapter 6

- Of the major metropolitan areas we examined, 40 have experienced housing price increases of at least 35 percent in the last five years, during a period of very modest general inflation.
- Only one community of those we examined, San Jose, California, had a housing price decline in the last 12 months.
- It appears that many of those cities with the highest-priced homes five years ago experienced, on average, the greatest price appreciation over the next five years.

- San Francisco, California, has the highest-price homes in the country with an average sales price of $530,900.
- San Diego, California, has the highest-priced homes relative to average household incomes. Many cities examined have a housing-to-income multiple far in excess of three times, a number that is considered safe by many lenders.
- In the last two years, national home prices have tripled the rate of growth of household incomes.
- Looking at housing prices relative to apartment building prices is an innovative way to see if your city's homes are overvalued relative to the rental market.

C H A P T E R

Similarities to Other Spectacular Crashes

Can We Learn from Our Mistakes?

The reader may remain generally skeptical, even after having seen the actual housing pricing data presented and reading the theoretical arguments. A skeptic might say, "Theoretically speaking, I see how some nonmarket forces are driving prices upward, but what are the chances that it will result in a market crash?" We read interesting theories about housing being overvalued, but when we go home at night the house is still there and the family dog still greets us as he always did. In other words, our everyday experience and exposure to such high home prices familiarizes us to a level of lofty prices that directly contradicts this book's findings. What are you going to believe, your own eyes or some book you read? It takes a very strong unbiased person to remember how overpriced we thought homes were 10 years ago when they sold at half of today's values!

To show you that such periods of overvaluation and aggressiveness eventually get corrected, here is my summary of five other market crashes that I happen to have lived through, and survived. It is to be hoped that you will begin to see similarities between these rather catastrophic events and the current housing market that will motivate you to take actions to protect your family's net worth. So here we go with "What Were They Thinking?"

The 1987 Stock Market Crash

I arrived on Wall Street in 1981 and immediately felt the brunt of a major recession as Reagan tried to curtail the inflationary effects of the government's having printed excessive amounts of currency. As he adopted a policy of borrowing to fund deficits, rather than printing money, inflation came under control and the country took off on a six-year economic expansion.

It was not until October 1987 that members of my generation saw their first real stock market crash. In one day the Dow dropped some 20 percent, causing people to run to their windows, not to jump, but just to see if the other guy was. In the late afternoon of the day of the crash, I got up from my desk on the investment-banking floor and went down and sat on our arbitrage desk on the equity-trading floor. Bob Rubin, the partner in charge of arbitrage at the time and future Secretary of the Treasury for the United States, was out of town on business, so the task of managing our $320 million arbitrage account fell to a young contemporary of mine, Frank Brosens.

Arbitrage, by definition, is supposed to be riskless trading based on mathematical relationships between selected securities. At an investment bank, it represents all of the firm's proprietary trading done for the firm's own account on behalf of its partners or shareholders. Gains and losses go directly to the partners or shareholders and trades are executed on their behalf, not on behalf of any client of the firm. Typically, there are arbitrage programs involving convertible securities and dividend payment dates, but in 1987, at the height of the 1980s merger boom, most of our positions, as well as those of other investment banks on the street, involved betting that announced corporate mergers would close on time and with at least the price announced being paid out.

Arbitrage desks, as well as many independent hedge funds, would invest in the stocks of companies that were the announced targets of merger bids. The market price of the target would lag the announced deal price, reflecting some uncertainty that the deal would be financed and closed, as well as the time value of money needed to make it worth your while to invest today and wait to get your merger check in the future. Initially, this price discount was substantial and big profits were made by the participants. Occasionally, they received a windfall profit if a third bidder emerged and a bidding war erupted. But, over time, the discount and profit potential nearly evaporated. Deals were trading at very small or no discounts at all to the announced deal price. At the time we thought the investors were crazy, but later we found out that they were playing with other people's money, utilizing incredible amounts of leverage. Putting these security investments in many different baskets allowed the investors to escape with most of their net worth if there was a collapse and leave the bank that extended them the credit holding the bag.

I watched in horror as Frank tallied the day's losses on the firm's $320 million portfolio. In one day the firm had lost $140 million! Frank's $320 million portfolio, marked to market, was now worth $180 million.

Like all good stories, this one had a happy ending. Frank and I stayed up until midnight trying to figure out if any of the firms we had sold stock to would still be in business in five days when it came time to settle the trade and pay us. Bob Rubin came back the next morning and, in one of the most commanding examples of leadership I have witnessed in my life, asked Frank if he thought the world was ending. Frank said no, so they started buying again and recovered most of their losses as the market slowly crawled back.

Now there have been academic studies on this day in history that purport to show that the initial cause of the day's festivities originally occurred in the Far East in early, early trading. We don't dispute that there may have been bad news coming out of Asia, and that an Asian market downturn may have triggered things in the United States. But, I know that what caused the severity of the crash was a bubble of irrational prices, based on a history of enormous profit taking, in a business few clearly understood, being played with enormous amounts of leverage and other people's money. That highly leveraged business was merger arbitrage and I know it was the culprit behind the crash because I witnessed it firsthand.

The 1990 Leveraged Buyout Crash

In 1984, I was asked to be a founding member of our firm's Leveraged Buyout Group. These LBOs were a relatively new phenomena. KKR and Forstmann Little were the pioneers of the technique in which business managements could borrow huge sums of moneys, without recourse to them personally but based on valuation appraisals of a business, and use the moneys to buy their businesses and take them private. The non-recourse nature of the loans meant that the banks could not come after the managers' personal assets if there was a problem with the loan. If successful, the cash flow from the business paid down the debt over time, making the managers enormously wealthy.

In the early eighties, LBOs were being accomplished with debt equal to three to six times cash flow. Managers became wealthy, banks collected enormous fees, and arrangers like KKR took a percentage of the profits equal to billions of dollars.

As in any competitive market when such huge profit potential exists, many new participants tried to join the party. Bidding for companies that wished to accomplish LBOs escalated to where successful bids involved debt equal to 9 to 12 times cash flow. Riskier and riskier securities were created. Drexel Burnham found a natural use for its junk bond product as the most subordinated form of debt in these LBO capital structures. My favorite phrase from the period was printed on the cover of many of Drexel's junk bonds, and I paraphrase—Management does not expect to earn sufficient cash flow from the business to cover its interest expenses and at the present time does not foresee the possibility of ever repaying the principal. Although I paraphrased for effect, the actual wording was not that different. Today, it sounds as if I am kidding, but at the height of junk bond mania, the issuers were very, very serious. You might ask who would be crazy enough to buy a bond with that kind of warning, but remember that these bonds had coupon yields of over 15 percent and also remember that people still smoke cigarettes despite the warning on the package.

Like all good parties, this one was due to end. Very unsophisticated lending and arranging institutions had entered the market, and deals were getting done at higher and higher prices, utilizing more and more leverage. LBOs are the quintessential use of leverage and other people's money. Some deals were done with less that 1 percent equity, or more than 99 percent debt, and many deals were completed with managements getting between 10 and 20 percent of the company's equity for free.

If you had to pick one deal that signaled the end was near, it had to be RJR Nabisco. The details of the infighting between the greedy LBO arrangers can be found in the book *Barbarians at the Gate,* by Bryan Burrough and John Helyar, which was made into a movie. It is a difficult movie to watch because you want to root for the good guy, if you could only find one. Driven by greed, each of the competing parties offered higher and higher prices, only to have the final price reach a debt burden equal to 18 times cash flow. And this, just so a management team could produce cigarettes and get rich off their sickly and addicted customers. KKR won the bidding, and in maybe the greatest Pyrrhic victory ever, ended up losing more of its investors' money in this one deal than they had earned them in all of their previous LBOs combined. Such is often the end result of betting the ranch and continuing to double down when you are playing with the house's money.

The 1990 Commercial Real Estate Crash

The crash of the LBO market caused such losses at our commercial banks that they started a general retrenchment in all their lending activities. The 1990 recession, which was partly caused by this bank retrenchment, contributed greatly to the banks' problems. The banks' loan problems were most clearly evident in the commercial real estate market. The greatest symbols of excessive building in this market were the "see-throughs" of Houston, Texas—brand-new glass office buildings that had no tenants, no curtains, and no furniture. Travelers on Houston's extensive freeway system could quite easily view numerous buildings that they could literally see through.

In the 1980s real estate developers had taken advantage of a tight market for office space and ever-increasing office rents to begin to build properties on spec with no long-term occupant commitments. Once again, banks lent up to 100 percent of the construction costs in hopes that they would be taken out by a permanent financing arrangement when the building was completed and tenant contracts were signed. The magic of this boom was that many developers were able to participate with zero money down. The degree of leverage and debt on the properties was enormous. Donald Trump, the New York real estate tycoon, got so leveraged at one point that his properties had to go up 10 percent in value each year so that he could refinance every year and use the increase in price to pay the interest on his debt. I believe this is the only known case in history in which a lending program had more than 100 percent debt in its capital structure!

The 1993–1994 Stock Market and Commercial Real Estate Crashes in Japan

Maybe the most spectacular crash of my generation occurred in the Japanese property and stock markets in 1993-1994. Tokyo stocks and real estate had achieved astronomical valuations by the beginning of the nineties. Some areas of downtown Tokyo had land selling for over $22,000 per square foot (about the size of an unfolded dinner napkin), and the Japanese stock market had a P/E attached to it that could only be justified if Japan had a real growth rate of at least 15 percent for the next 40 years. But people, especially Americans far from the action, took great comfort in the fact that these were market-derived prices; as unbelievable as they might seem, they must be right. What follows is a first-hand description of this so-called market.

I visited Tokyo in 1991. As part of my tour we visited the stock exchange and I was escorted up to the second floor balcony overlooking the trading floor. Much to my surprise, and unlike the chaotic trading of the New York Stock Exchange, trading on the floor of the Japanese exchange was very orderly and revolved around only four large desks or counters that took up the entire room. I was told that each of these desks represented one of the elite trading companies in Japan: Nomura, Nikko, Daiwa, and Yamaichi. Unlike American exchanges in which trading occurs at hundreds of posts, in Tokyo all trading occurs through one of four gigantic trading firms.

As if this were not enough cause for concern, in the middle of each desk was a bright red telephone, one on each of the four major desks.

When I asked, I was told that each phone was a direct line to the Ministry of Finance. It was apparent that rather than having the cumulative effect of many small trades dictate the direction of the day's market; here a phone call from the government would decide winners and losers. Japan was an autocratic government with pricing largely determined by its government, its banks, and its largest companies, but beautifully disguised as a market economy. Not only were businesses and banks able to push stock and land prices to higher and higher levels, but when the crash came in 1993, the regulators and the government never insisted that the banks write off their bad loans. Instead the banks were allowed to pull back on their productive commercial lending and just invest in low-risk government securities until they earned enough to offset their loan losses. Unfortunately, this process has taken nine years so far and is the major reason Japan has gone from being a major economic world player to being an economic also-ran. (Of the four large trading houses that I saw back in 1991 on the floor of the Tokyo exchange, only Nomura remains today as a stand-alone company. Yamaichi has gone bankrupt and the other two houses were consumed in larger mergers.)

Japanese businesses during the boom years invested in other companies' stocks, made speculative real estate investments, and increased worldwide trading revenues, but not necessarily their profitability. They ended up buying up much of the commercial real estate in Los Angeles, Texas, and New York, but at ridiculously hard-to-justify prices. When a gentleman that I met on an airplane heard that I worked on Wall Street, he accused me of selling our country out to the Japanese. I said that this might be true, but he should know we were getting awfully good prices for it. After the eventual crash, cash-poor Japanese companies ended up liquidating many of their American investments for half or even less of what they had paid for them.

The 2000 Technology Stock Crash

Each of the crashes that we have described so far involved transactions in an economic environment that did not fully satisfy the requirements of being a "market economy." In each case the financing institutions provided the majority of the investment capital, principals played with little to none of their own capital at risk, and there was not a plethora of active and willing buyers and sellers. This cannot be said for the Internet stock crash of 2000 and 2001. These stocks were priced and traded in the most sophisticated market in the world, with great access to liquidity and general agreement each and every day from hundreds of millions of investors that while obviously high, these stocks deserved their astronomical valuations. It is difficult to explain how such an efficient market as the technology-laden Nasdaq index could collapse from a high of over 5000 in March 2000 to near 1100 in October 2002.

What is most disturbing to me is that such events could have occurred in what we thought was a fairly sophisticated market. Of course, there is the view that there was a chance that Internet companies would take over the world and bankrupt all existing bricks-and-mortar businesses. I guess if this had occurred we would have been talking about how undervalued the Internet stocks looked in the beginning of the year 2000. Eduardo Schwartz of UCLA made this point in an academic paper in which he argued that utilizing option theory, Internet valuations at their peak seemed to make sense as an option on supernormal performance.

It would be very easy to Monday morning quarterback the collapse of Internet stocks, as many pundits are currently doing. It is amusing that many of these television commentators were the same ones who had been promoting stocks trading at multiples equal to hundreds of times their sales level. P/Es were an antiquated concept, as most Internet companies had no earnings. The only reason I feel somewhat justified in my critique is that I published a book before the crash that made the same points I will make now. What I said in 1999 before the crash was not based on macroeconomic or financial ratio analysis but rather on a back-of-the-envelope analysis of competitive business strategy.

The first point I made in 1999 was that many Internet companies seemed overly dependent on proceeds from banner advertisements on their site for the majority of their projected revenues. I met a gentleman who told me that you could buy 1000 banner ad placements, to be placed at very reputable Internet sites, for a total of five cents. I spent the next half hour checking my math because if that was the market rate for Internet banner ads, and I wanted to spend $1.5 million, or about the cost of a 30-second television commercial during the Super Bowl, I would be able to buy 30 billion banner ads on the best sites on the Internet. Clearly, if Yahoo and others were banking on big banner ad revenues, the current pricing system was going to have to change.

The second point I made was that although it was true that the Internet was a boon to consumers and that eventually some Internet companies' revenues would be enormous, because there were no barriers to competition, it was hard for me to envision them ever making much in the way of profits. The simple analogy I gave was something related to spider technology. Spiders are virtual programs that can go comparison-shopping for you. In effect, there should come a time when just before you are ready to purchase a book from Amazon for $24.95, up will pop your spider on your screen with the Web address of a virtual bookstore that will sell you the same book for $21.95. It is hard to imagine many Amazon customers maintaining such store loyalty so as to miss an opportunity to save $3, especially since they have never met the store manager at Amazon, never tried their coffee, and never sat on a Sunday afternoon in one of their recliners reading their magazines.

My final concern about the unsustainability of high Internet stock prices concerned the Ponzi nature of the investment. Great Ponzi schemes work, not based on imagined payoffs like a lottery might, but real actual payoffs to the original investors that can be witnessed, driven, or lived in. Internet investors all witnessed each day the real returns their fellow investors were receiving from the market in the form of new expensive cars parked in the company parking lot, beautiful new homes bought with trading profits, or new sailboats with names like Day Trader or OPM (for Other People's Money). To ignore such real evidence is contrary to everything we are taught about how to make effective decisions. But it is exactly this type of physical evidence such as big home values that homeowners must discount if they are to uncover the true value of their property. Remember when your home was worth half what it is today, and you thought it was very highly valued even then. What does that say about today's value? Great investors have wonderful memories and put current market conditions in historical context easily.

Conclusion

So looking at the recent history of five great bubbles and crashes, we would have to conclude that bubbles and crashes are definitely possible, and that their likelihood increases dramatically as conditions appear to resemble less and less true "market" conditions. Limited participants playing with other people's money, in a constantly increasing price environment, with lots of debt leverage provided by aggressive but relatively uninformed bankers, who do not book the assets on their balance sheets, lead to eventual bubbles, crashes, and taxpayer bailouts. Unfortunately, today's residential real estate market has many of these dangerous ingredients and could be cooking up a real kitchen explosion.

Summary of Chapter 7

- An examination of other recent crashes highlights similarities with the current housing market. Namely, we looked at the 1987 stock market crash, the 1990 LBO crash, the 1990 commercial real estate crash, the 1993–1994 Japanese stock market and real estate crashes, as well as the crash of U.S. technology stocks in 2000.
- Each major crash involved a great deal of financial leverage with principals playing with other people's money.
- Banks, bank fees, bank employees' motivations, and banks' inability to manage risk all played an important role in each of the crashes.
- Government involvement and assurances in a number of these instances prevented participants from properly evaluating and reacting to risk.
- Often unusually high prices before the crash were justified by people who said that the old rules no longer applied and that we were entering a new paradigm of how to determine values.
- Many of these markets were not real economic markets as they actually had very few participants whose downside risk was limited by others or by third-party guarantees.
- Common sense was displaced by an attitude that everyone was making money, I was not going to be left out, and there will always be a greater fool to sell to down the road.

C H A P T E R 8

How Will It Begin?

We are living in an unusual time. It is the best of times and it is the worst of times. Many Americans are enjoying a standard of living unattainable by many on the planet. There is still substantial poverty in the country and incomes seem to be bifurcating, but we have enjoyed a dramatic increase in prosperity over the last 20 years. People are working hard, and as we have seen, in many families both parents must work in order to pay the mortgage.

Storm Warnings

But there are storm warnings on the horizon. Government's having gotten too cozy with business has resulted in lax accounting oversight and weakened business regulation that has damaged investors' confidence in the market. Interest rates are at 40-year lows, and yet there is little pickup in business activity. With short rates near 1 percent, the tried-and-true formula for stimulating the economy by just cutting interest rates is beginning to make less and less sense. Similarly, the rule of cutting taxes to stimulate the economy is harder to follow in a world of trillion-dollar deficits. Huge windfalls have already been generated for the wealthiest in the form of reduced income taxes, capital gains tax cuts, inheritance tax cuts, and the government's having made it easier for U.S. businesses to relocate off-shore and avoid all taxes. Governments do not seem to have the desire or capacity to spend us out of recession, business is reducing its investments, and consumers, as we have noted earlier, are up to their eyeballs in debt.

The world is looking to the U.S. market as the driving consumer force supporting enormous worldwide production. Japan still is not growing, due mostly to the inability of its government to deal with bad loan problems at its largest banks. Japan is the classic example of what can go wrong when government gets too close to business. At one time admired for finding a new paradigm of business and government cooperation, Japan's system has now been exposed for what it is, corrupt cronyism. Europe is doing well, but has its hands full in incorporating the eastern European countries into the European Community, with the eventual planned admittance of Turkey and Russia expected soon thereafter.

Although we cannot predict the future and have always avoided the opportunity to guess interest rates or stock market movements, the future's impact on the housing market can be determined without any prior fortune-telling experience. The reason is quite simple. I will show that regardless of whether interest rates increase or decrease in the future, it will be bad for housing prices. If rates increase, it will be a sign of increased business activity, or it may signal a return of inflation if our government stupidly starts printing money to fund our deficits. Either way, we would expect housing prices to suffer if rates increase. The reason is that new homebuyers would qualify for significantly lower sums of home financing, even if their incomes remained the same. A small increase in wages of say 3 to 5 percent from a stronger economy would be dwarfed in the lenders' qualifying formula if rates increased from 6 to 8 percent (a 25 percent increase in rate levels from the formula's perspective).

If rates decrease in the future, things also look quite bleak for housing. While the qualifying formula will justify higher and higher amounts of leverage, we would expect foreclosures and bankruptcies to explode. The reason is that if long Treasury rates drop below 3 percent, there is a high likelihood of a deflationary spiral, a danger we have not faced in this country since the Great Depression. Supposedly, we learned our lesson during that depression that we should not tighten money supply in a recession, but given the current policies of an always inflation-fighting Fed, that might be exactly what they end up doing. If it happens, it will send our economists scrambling for their college textbooks as no one has dealt with deflation in generations and no one has a good idea as to how to handle it.

Let us look at these two scenarios to see how the housing crash might begin. Then we will look at two other important, but less likely events, that could send housing into a tailspin. The housing market is already starting to weaken. Many of the most overpriced metropolitan markets have begun to show weakened sales activity. Nationwide, the number of single-family homes on the market and available for sale has increased from 1.7 million in 1999 to over 2.2 million in 2002.

What If Rates Increase?

If interest rates increase in the future, people will end up qualifying for less and less mortgage financing. It will be bad for housing prices, regardless of whether the increase in rates is a real increase, signaling a healthier economy and a desire on behalf of business for increased levels of investment activity, or whether the rate increase is nominal, resulting from government's return to an inflationary money supply policy. If rates increase, amounts that new homebuyers qualify for will decline. How will home prices sustain if new buyers qualify for 20 percent less mortgage money? We doubt buyers will invest any additional equity in their home purchases. We doubt their incomes will be much higher. We doubt they will be willing to place any other family members in servitude, slaving to pay the mortgage, given that both parents are already working. Asking the kids to deliver newspapers to help pay the mortgage seems extreme, as does insisting Grandmamma pay up or shut up!

So, if we are right, and here we are only talking about the scenario in which rates increase, housing prices will fall. What is fascinating about this is that most families have locked in their mortgage interest rates for 30 years. Thus we have seen that they are quite smug about the fact that rate increases will not be able to hurt them. Before we attack this smugness, let us look at those who better not be smug: ARM borrowers.

ARM borrowers have a great deal to worry about if rates increase. We pointed out previously that even though they are limited by rate movement caps, these caps represent a much bigger percentage of their total mortgage interest rate than historically. A 3 percent cap on rate movements when rates are at 4 percent represents a much larger potential increase in mortgage payments (75 percent) than the same cap when rates are at 12 percent (25 percent). This means that over a couple of years, recent ARM borrowers could find their monthly mortgage payments more than doubled. Now most homebuyers understood this risk and properly locked in rates at the time of their home purchase. Still, some 20 percent of new buyers and approximately 10 percent of all outstanding mortgages are ARMs. These seem like small numbers until you remember we are dealing with a $5.7 trillion home mortgage market. This means that there are over $500 billion in ARMs outstanding. This is a bigger value than the market capitalization of any single company on the New York Stock Exchange!

The *Wall Street Journal* reported on October 7, 2002, that the percentage of new homebuyers utilizing ARMs is increasing. The percentage of new homebuyers utilizing ARMs has increased to 20 percent from 10 percent in 2001, according to the Federal Housing Finance Board. This might seem counterintuitive as rates are at an all-time low and the timing seems ideal to lock in a fixed rate on one's mortgage. The article surmises that some buyers are being forced to choose houses beyond their means, and in order to afford the monthly mortgage payment they are agreeing to the riskier floating rate of an ARM rather than a higher fixed rate mortgage. This is a recipe for disaster, as those most stretched financially will have the riskiest, most variable mortgage payment to fund.

If $500 billion of ARM home mortgages get into trouble and threaten default, it would have enormous ramifications to the economy. First, mortgage holders would take a financial beating. Insurance companies, public and private pension funds, and municipal governments all hold mortgage pass-through securities in their portfolios and would suffer enormously. We shall see in the next chapter what damage could occur if Fannie Mae and Freddie Mac suffer significant losses in their rather substantial mortgage portfolios.

Individual banks would have to claim significant loan losses if ARM defaults increase. This might cause them to reduce their exposure in general and be less aggressive in home lending as well as other types of lending. Their pullback in home lending would only exacerbate a bad situation, as their qualifying formulas in the higher rate environment would also be directing them to be less aggressive. In addition to the rate increases, initial defaults by ARM borrowers will result in reduced lending by banks to new homebuyers, putting a lid on home price appreciation in general. As banks foreclose on defaulting ARM' borrowers, their inventory of foreclosed properties will put a real damper on the prices of homes in every community. Banks do not hold onto foreclosed properties for long, and there is nothing worse than trying to sell your house when a bank is liquidating a similar property down the street at 70 cents on the dollar.

So, you might ask, what does this all mean to me? I am a homeowner, but I locked in my mortgage rate for 30 years and I'm not planning on selling any time soon. So what if a rate increase slows new home buying, bankrupts some ARM borrowers, or depresses home prices? Well, the answer is that the depressed home prices could have a very real effect on the economy.

First, there is a wealth effect on consumption. When people feel wealthier, either from increases in their stock portfolio or from increases in the values of their homes, they tend to spend more. This has very real effects on the health of an economy. Economists have found that people spend more of each dollar of appreciation in their homes than in their stock portfolios because they seem to view the price increase as more permanent, because their homes are much more leveraged, and because there are many available methods to borrow against increased home prices, including second mortgages and home equity loans. *Fortune* magazine on October 28, 2002, reported that economists John Quigley of Berkeley, Robert Shiller of Yale, and Karl Case of Wellesley showed that for every $1000 a house appreciates, homeowners spend $60, or 0.6 percent. This compares with 0.3 percent for stock market increases.

Fortune also reported that in 2001 and 2002, homeowners took $350 billion in cash out of their houses through refinancings and home equity loans. (In November of 2002, *USA Today* reported that economy.com expected the total to be closer to $420 billion for the two years combined.) So far they have spent some $70 billion on consumption goods that has helped to prop up the economy in a recession. The Federal Reserve estimates that they will use $120 billion to pay down credit card and other consumer debt. That leaves $165 billion still unspent. Not only would this consumption activity stop if home prices fell, but it would reverse itself as homeowners would have to consume less in order to feel comfortable with their reduced housing net worths.

Second, if home prices fall, it could have a very real effect directly on the economy. The reason is that if a significant percentage of homeowners find themselves living in an underwater asset, then labor mobility could be disrupted. As we said earlier, an asset is considered underwater when its total debts exceed its market value. This shouldn't make a difference to the long-term holder, but it becomes a real problem for someone wishing to sell his home in order to take a new job in a new town or someone who must sell to face a financial crisis such as job loss, medical problems, or divorce. The inability of people to sell their homes easily to take on better job opportunities has a dramatic impact on labor mobility. Labor mobility is something we have come to take for granted in our economy, but without it an economy suffers terribly. Real growth is almost impossible without labor mobility. Job shuffling is the physical manifestation of the economic principle of employing all labor resources at their most efficient allocation. If labor mobility suffers, recessions are likely to be prolonged.

So, even though many current homeowners have no present plans to sell their homes, the combined effects of an interest rate increase could be devastating to them. Rate increases could cause ARM mortgage defaults, reduced labor mobility, general bank retrenchment, and lower housing prices, all with rather devastating effects on the general economy. As the general economy softens, more traditional sources of home mortgage defaults will occur as people begin to lose their jobs. This will further dampen housing prices.

In writing this chapter I am reminded of what we used to call the pessimistic chief economist at Salomon Brothers. He was known as Dr. Death because he always found reasons to foretell economic doom, bad for the stock market but very good for Salomon's bond customers. While I hope I may earn a more cheery appellation in life, I feel I have to call it like I see it. If I am doomed to a life of responding to terms of endearment involving disfigurement and death, at least I will know I earned them by telling the truth as I saw it about a very serious problem in our country.

What If Rates Declined?

Let us now examine what would happen if rates decreased in the future. With the 10-year Treasury rate at 4 percent, mortgage rates at a 40-year low of 6 percent, and the short-term Fed Funds rate set by the Fed at 1.25 percent, it is hard to imagine them heading much lower. It is true that mortgage rates are, historically speaking, at a relatively big spread to the 10-year Treasury, so if rates settled here, mortgage rates might tighten and their yield drop a bit more. But the real question is whether long Treasury yields can head further south. The 10-year Treasury's lowest yield was 3.6 percent in the fall of 2002, but it didn't stay there long before increasing.

What could cause rates to head lower from such historically low levels? Recently, rates have been driven lower by the Federal Reserve Board. The Fed has lowered the Fed Funds rate from 5 percent on March 20, 2001, to 1.25 percent on November 6, 2002, through a series of nine separate rate cuts. The Fed Funds rate is an overnight rate at which banks that are members of the Federal Reserve can theoretically borrow from the Federal Reserve. While it influences how the market sets long-term rates, it is not the sole determinant. The bond market makes its own determination of what it believes will be the long-term inflation rate and growth in the economy, and then allows supply and demand to set long rates. To the extent that the Fed has greatly influenced long rates in the past, obviously with the Fed Funds rate now at 1.25 percent, they have much less dry powder to work with. Is there really a business out there that will increase its investments in a 1 percent Fed Funds interest rate environment that would not have already done so at 1.25 percent?

Historically, people have assumed that the "real" component of interest rates, after accounting for inflation, is approximately 3 percent per year. This means that a 4 percent Treasury rate implies a 1 percent inflation rate. So for rates to trend lower, either people have to presume that we will not be in a normal economy sufficient to generate 3 percent real returns, or people will have to be forecasting a period of deflation. For obvious reasons, it would not be beneficial to the housing market if we were to go into a more permanent, low-growth recessionary environment. Associated job losses would greatly increase foreclosures and put large amounts of foreclosed properties on the market at fairly depressed prices. We should discuss why a period of deflation could be equally, if not more, damaging.

By definition, housing prices are probably going to decline in a deflation. But if they did no worse than all other goods, it would not be considered a real price decline. We have seen that inflation is good for the tax avoidance ability of home mortgage borrowers. Similarly, low inflation or deflation would minimize the value of this tax advantage. Homeowners would be unwilling to lose money on their house investment every year for a minimal interest expense deduction from their taxes.

The real risk of a deflationary environment is that prices and wages do not adjust smoothly. People are slow to take the necessary wage cuts needed to "keep up" with deflation. Wages become sticky and unemployment escalates. Such problems can lead to a degenerating spiral in the economy that has a terrible consequence; once it starts it is very difficult to stop. Once businesses, consumers, and workers lose confidence in an economy, it is very hard to re-instill that confidence. Employers do not hire, consumers do not spend, and businesses do not invest, and this logjam cannot be broken. Obviously, such a weakened economy would have dramatic negative consequences to home prices, as job losses, defaults, foreclosures, and personal bankruptcies would escalate dramatically. For a review of what happened in the deflationary environment of the Great Depression, I would guide the reader to Milton Friedman's excellent text, *A Monetary History of the United States, 1867–1960*.

There is a second compounding effect during deflationary periods. We saw earlier that we were surprised at the increasing number of mortgage foreclosures given that home prices have been steadily increasing recently. It would have seemed much more logical for individual homeowners to sell and pay off the debt in an environment of ever-increasing prices than allow the bank to foreclose and lose their equity in the home. Obviously, average home prices do not tell the story for all members of a community.

But now imagine what would happen in a deflationary period. The regular price declines of all goods, including homes, would prevent a troubled homeowner from selling at a profit and repaying his mortgage. Instead, the number of foreclosures would escalate, even if the price declines were not real but solely due to general deflation. Therefore, another unanticipated shortcoming of a deflationary period is that foreclosures in all asset classes should increase, which cannot be good for the economy or the housing market.

Two More Warnings

There are two other "events" that, while less likely than rate increases or declines, should be discussed because they would have very real impacts on housing prices. First, we have seen that 10 to 30 percent of the value of a home depends on the homeowner's ability to deduct interest expenses from his primary residence mortgage against his income taxes. In a world of increasing federal deficits, there will be increased talk of how to raise more funds for the government, either through direct tax increases or the elimination of popular deductions. Given the current administration's professed desire to lower taxes on wealthy individuals and businesses, the middle class better watch out. The home mortgage interest deductibility is held so dearly by homeowners that it could only be attacked as part of a major tax reorganization. Movements toward a one-rate tax system or the reduction of mortgage interest deductibility could both be methods employed to further tax the middle class.

Second, something completely unrelated to the housing market could have a negative effect on home prices. If banks suffered significant loan losses in any of their other businesses, they could react by retrenching in all their lending activities. When this happens the areas most affected will be those geographic regions most directly affected by the loan problem: New York City if it's business financing–related, Seattle if it's aircraft leasing, or maybe Dallas and Houston if the oil fields take a hit. There could be a fallout nationally in the housing market if banks become less aggressive in lending generally. All bank practices would be reexamined under such a scenario, and mortgage lending would come under increased scrutiny because it involves high leverage and aggressive bank tactics and terms. If banks pulled back on the aggressive terms that they have been willing to lend under, you should expect that new homebuyers would be able to borrow less and home prices would decline. Such a price decline would then trigger many of the bad outcomes mentioned above.

Where Will It All Start?

In an article in the September 3, 2001, issue titled "What If Housing Crashed?" *Forbes* magazine reported that there is generally a lag between the time an economy softens and the time that housing prices come under pressure. The article examined the impact on housing prices in three metropolitan markets that experienced difficult periods in their recent past. Boston, the article said, was achieving record home prices in 1987, just as the "Massachusetts Miracle" of high-tech business on Route 128 was running out of steam. Many high-tech firms in the area were suffering, including Apollo, Wang, Digital, and Lotus, and 27,000 people lost their jobs. However, it was not until 1990 that housing prices began their descent, ending up 20 percent lower in real terms, after inflation.

Forbes reported that Wall Street lost 30,000 jobs after the market crash of 1987, but it was not until 1993 that home prices reached their nadir, some 23 percent below their 1989 levels in real terms. Houston had experienced a decade-long oil boom when oil prices peaked in 1981 at $35 per barrel. Housing prices stayed high as oil prices collapsed, reaching $9 per barrel in 1986. Then, the article reported, home values began their descent and by 1988 had given back all of their earlier gains. Clearly, there is evidence that home price declines lag behind economic downturns because people are slow to sell their homes and recognize their losses.

John Cassidy wrote a compelling piece titled "The Next Crash" on the threat of a housing price collapse in *The New Yorker* on November 11, 2002. He quotes Christopher Wood, a financial analyst at C.L.S.A. Emerging Markets, a brokerage and investment bank: "In a real estate crash, the top end of the market usually cracks first. Then the bad news escalates down." Cassidy reports that in 1989, at the peak of the last real estate boom, Wood advised his New York friends to sell their apartments and rent for a year. Wood is issuing the same advice again. He says, "The

American housing market is the last big bubble. When it bursts, it will be very ugly. In places like Manhattan and San Francisco, prices could easily drop 40 or 50 percent."

Cassidy points out that homebuyers today seem to have forgotten what happened when the property boom of the eighties came to an end. He says between 1989 and 1995, inflation-adjusted house prices in San Francisco and San Jose fell by almost 40 percent. In Honolulu, the downturn lasted a full decade: between the second quarter of 1991 and the first quarter of 2001, the real price of houses fell by almost a third.

In October 2002 the *Wall Street Journal* reported that the very high end of the residential real estate market was already showing signs of stress cracks. They reported that superpriced homes, with sales prices exceeding $10 million, are in the middle of an unprecedented glut. According to one count, there are at least 44 houses for sale across the country with asking prices over $20 million, up from just 11 homes for sale at that price point five years ago. A record dozen homes were on the market at prices exceeding $50 million. They ask if a bubble can burst from the top. In the post–Gulf War slump, high-priced homes tumbled first and farthest, with prices falling as much as 50 percent in places like Bel-Air, California.

The *Wall Street Journal* also reported that much of the demand for homes is now coming from speculators and investors who pulled their money out of the stock market, rather than from families who intend to occupy the homes for years at a time. They cited that *Flipping Properties,* a guide to making money in real estate investments, had reached the Top 100 sellers list on Amazon.com.

Realtors and mortgage bankers like to talk about the tightness of supply and demand for housing to argue that home prices will continue their upward trend. They point to the number of immigrants coming into the country as causing an ever-increasing demand for homes. What they forget to tell you is that most of the baby boomers have already purchased their homes. Demographically speaking, this was the big wave of demand for housing that needed satisfying, and it was handled by record levels of new home construction across the nation.

The other "source" of housing supply that is never discussed is the 21.5 million homes in America that are owned by individuals at least 65 years old. This is approximately 20 percent of all U.S. households.

Regardless of whether these older Americans sell to third parties and move into assisted living arrangements or leave their homes in their estate planning to their relatives and friends, this will ease any tightness in the housing market for the foreseeable future.

If you have found this discussion a bit depressing, or if you suffer from a weak heart, we advise you to skip the next chapter in which we discuss what might happen if things really go bad. If you can believe it, to date, we have just discussed the tip of a very deep and cold iceberg. While the discussion in this chapter entails events that are very likely, such as interest rate increases and declines, events in the next chapter will hopefully not unfold unless we are very, very unlucky or very, very stupid.

Summary of Chapter 8

- Our economy is in difficult territory as the only force keeping it from dipping back into recession is consumer spending, which to a great degree is being fueled by money taken out of homes through refinancings and home equity loans.
- If rates increase, even if business activity picks up, housing prices will most likely head down as new homebuyers will qualify for much less mortgage financing and ARM borrowers will get into trouble with their increasing mortgage payments.
- If rates decrease, this could be the beginning of a deflationary spiral that would be very bad for the economy and home prices.
- Even if you have a fixed rate mortgage, a severe housing price correction could make it impossible for you to move if your house is worth less than your mortgage balance.
- This decrease in labor mobility, combined with the decrease in general consumption due to fewer refinancings, could lead to even lower home prices.
- Legislation directly attacking mortgage interest deductibility or banks losing their aggressiveness in mortgage lending could also have a negative impact on housing prices.
- Housing downturns typically lag behind general economic weakness, and often it is the priciest homes that start the price decline.

How Bad Can It Get?

For those of you willing to examine a worst-case alternative, this chapter presents a much more pessimistic scenario. Assume, for one of the reasons stated in the preceding chapter, that housing prices have declined dramatically across the country, say at least 15 to 20 percent in many metropolitan areas, and mortgage defaults and foreclosures have jumped.

Can the Banks Get in Trouble?

We have seen that in a healthy economy with ever-increasing home prices, 1.2 percent of mortgages have entered foreclosure; therefore, it would not seem unrealistic to see foreclosures of 5 percent if the economy heads lower and home prices decline. Remember, foreclosures are much more likely when prices decline because the alternative of selling at a profit and repaying the debt in full is taken off the table. This means an additional three million family homes may enter foreclosure with a total potential property loss of $100 billion. This could have devastating effects on the upstream holders and guarantors of residential mortgage debt in this country and on the country as a whole.

Figure 9.1 shows that the mortgage market has been subject to rather amazing growth over the past 20 years. Remember, as presented here mortgages are income-producing assets held for investment, not liabil-

ities as they are to homeowners. Since the demise of government-guar-
anteed 5.25 percent passbook savings accounts at savings and loans in
the seventies, S&Ls have accounted for a smaller and smaller percentage of the home mortgage business. S&Ls hold less than 12 percent of
total mortgage loans outstanding today.

Commercial banks, responsible for arranging many of the mortgages
outstanding today, end up holding only (only?) about $1.5 trillion. This
is a large number, but it is dominated by what federal agencies, like Ginnie Mae or quasi agencies like Fannie Mae and Freddie Mac, hold or
guarantee or what is sold to third-party investors as mortgage pass-
through securities. In Figure 9.1, we see a large amount of mortgage
pass-throughs or mortgage pools, but we shall see that a significant dollar amount of these securities are held by the respective agencies. For
ease of discussion, Fannie Mae and Freddie Mac will be called "agencies," but we will see that they are far from earning that moniker.

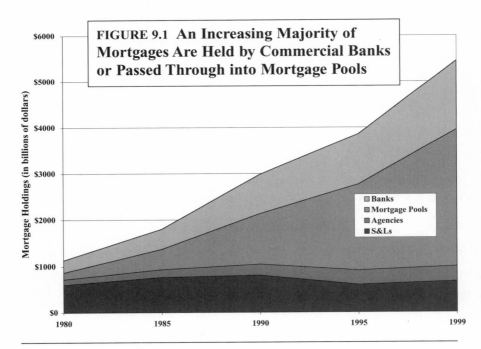

FIGURE 9.1 An Increasing Majority of Mortgages Are Held by Commercial Banks or Passed Through into Mortgage Pools

Source: Federal Reserve Board

The big change in the marketplace over the last 25 years has been the growth of the pass-through market. Mortgage pass-throughs provide incredible liquidity to a very long-term asset. Bankers are able to focus on origination without tying up their long-term capital. In essence, they package the mortgages and sell them to an institution more likely to want to invest for the long term, namely pension funds and life insurance companies. Traditionally invested in straight coupon bonds, these institutions insist that they not suffer high prepayment risk from the mortgages and that they have adequate guarantees or insurance against default. Mortgage insurance companies and mortgage packagers like Fannie Mae and Freddie Mac step in to play these roles. We will see that Fannie Mae and Freddie Mac end up holding a great deal more of these pass-through securities than we might like.

Figure 9.2 shows the residential mortgage holdings of all commercial banks in the country. The total mortgages on their books equaled

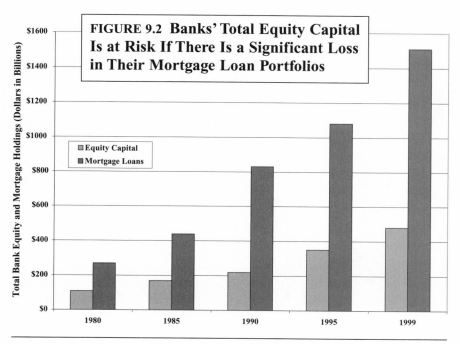

FIGURE 9.2 Banks' Total Equity Capital Is at Risk If There Is a Significant Loss in Their Mortgage Loan Portfolios

Source: U.S. Federal Deposit Insurance Corporation

$1.5 trillion at the end of 1999. In addition, the banks hold an additional $100 billion in home equity loans, which are much riskier loans than first-mortgage loans. To put this in perspective, I have plotted the total residential mortgage debt alongside the total equity capital for all banks in the country. You can see that just the home mortgage debt alone dwarfs the banks' total equity, ignoring all the other types of loans on the banks' books. If the banks lost 30 percent of the value of all their residential mortgage holdings it would wipe out the combined book equity of all the banks in the country. Now, we agree such a scenario is extremely unlikely, but the envisioned result is rather disturbing. For example, if they only lost 3 percent of their mortgage portfolio value, their equity accounts would take a 10 percent hit.

So, what are the risks that our banks could have a problem in their mortgage debt portfolios? Figure 9.3 demonstrates that banks are expe-

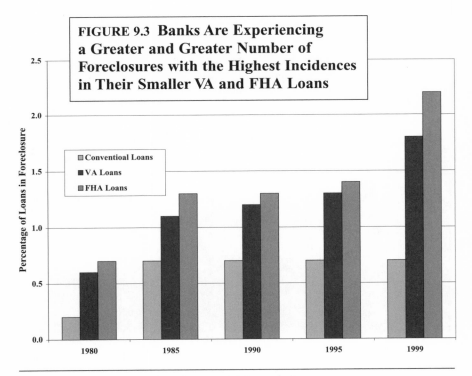

FIGURE 9.3 Banks Are Experiencing a Greater and Greater Number of Foreclosures with the Highest Incidences in Their Smaller VA and FHA Loans

Source: Mortgage Bankers Association, National Delinquency Survey

riencing higher and higher foreclosure rates, even during the healthiest housing market in history. As you would expect, their worst default experience is in their Veterans Administration and Federal Housing Administration loans, as these are typically smaller and appeal to homeowners of lower incomes. Figure 9.4 shows that banks have written off billions of bad loans in their overall lending portfolios in the last 20 years.

Figure 9.5 shows that banks have maintained their profitability by continuing to increase fees to their customers. Fees on ATM transactions are very popular, at least with bankers, with many banks charging their own customers double fees if they use some other bank's ATM machine. But fees in general have exploded with some banks charging you to talk to a teller, some charging $105 to bounce three $2 checks, and many charging lots of bizarre document and other esoteric fees to close a mortgage. Without this fee income, the banks' poor lending record would have driven their stock prices down substantially.

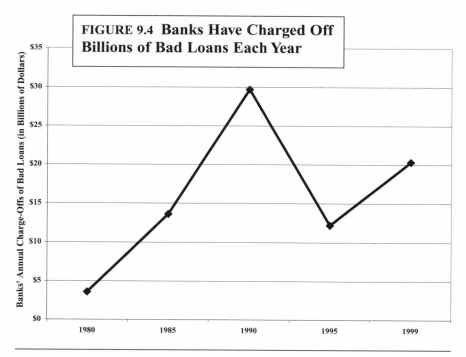

FIGURE 9.4 **Banks Have Charged Off Billions of Bad Loans Each Year**

Source: U.S. Federal Deposit Insurance Corporation

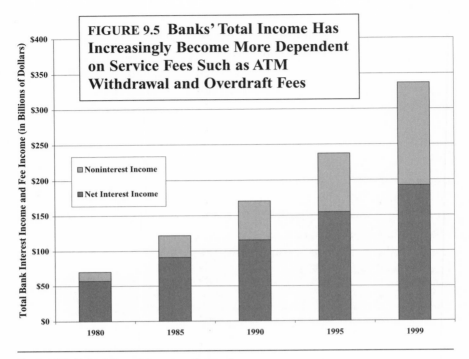

FIGURE 9.5 Banks' Total Income Has Increasingly Become More Dependent on Service Fees Such as ATM Withdrawal and Overdraft Fees

Source: U.S. Federal Deposit Insurance Corporation

The Role of Private Mortgage Insurance Providers

Banks, however, are not the institutions at greatest risk if there is a crash in housing prices. That honor goes to the smaller private mortgage insurance providers. Private mortgage insurance (PMI) providers are those insurance companies that guarantee investors that interest and principal will be paid in the event of a mortgage foreclosure or default. The PMI industry acts as a linchpin guaranteeing the safety of highly leveraged home mortgages as investments. Home mortgages have two big problems as investments: some of them are very highly levered, like 90 or 95 percent, and they always face the possibility of default and foreclosure. The PMI industry neatly solves both these problems for the investment community. It would be logical to assume that these are very large AAA-rated insurance companies since the risks and dollar amounts of potential liability that they are dealing with are so enormous. But, this is not always the case.

Over $750 billion of mortgages outstanding are covered by private mortgage insurance. These are the riskiest of mortgages because the homeowner typically puts less than 20 percent down at time of purchase, thus necessitating the need for private insurance. And yet, only two PMI companies are of a size to withstand any sizeable losses—AIG and GE Credit—and they control only approximately 30 percent of the total market for PMI.

The vast majority of the players in PMI are less than AAA-rated and are relatively small players in relation to the size of the risks they are underwriting. Five companies control a 70 percent market share, have insured mortgages totaling in excess of $530 billion, and yet have combined shareholder equity of only $11 billion. They are MGIC Corp., The PMI Group, Inc., Radian Group, Republic Insurance, and Triad Guaranty. How can five insurance companies with total equity of $11 billion survive if their $530 billion of residential mortgage debt starts to default? The simple answer is that they will not. The whole idea of insurance is for a very large substantial insurance company or group of companies to diversify risk across a broad portfolio of many types of assets. Here, 70 percent of the players are very small companies, with incredible leverage and risk exposure, insuring assets of only one kind—highly leveraged residential mortgages.

I am reminded of a particularly tough opinion letter that we as investment bankers were always asked to write to the board of directors of a company considering leveraging itself in an LBO. The board always needed written assurance that what we were recommending was a safe and sound idea. Well, neither we nor any of our competitors wanted to write such a guarantee, so a small company with almost no assets, which will remain nameless, became expert at crafting these letters. They charged $500,000 per page, and the joke went that they had their employees, their copying machines, and their typewriters all aboard a jet down at the airport in case anybody tried to collect on their guarantee. The idea of small companies making big insurance promises or guarantees is one of the dumber concepts we have seen in finance.

It is my opinion that if we have a meaningful increase in default rates due to a reduction in home prices, these smaller PMI insurers are in grave danger of collapsing. A 2 percent decline in the value of their mortgage insurance portfolio would reduce their book equity to zero. As an industry, they have already experienced increased defaults and delinquencies, especially in their sub-prime portfolio, and they have workout costs equal to approximately $30,000 for every mortgage that goes into foreclosure. Default rates will skyrocket if home prices decline and workout costs per foreclosure will at least double as liquidating underwater home property assets will be difficult to do in a down market.

The PMI business is not a healthy industry even now. It is very difficult for the participants to distinguish themselves other than through price-cutting. Because they do not control the distribution channel, these PMI providers have been forced to kick back about half of their premiums in the form of reinsurance to originators of mortgages. Homeowners have found a creative way to cut out the need for PMI altogether, even on highly levered mortgage transactions. Rather than do one 90 percent mortgage with required PMI, the homeowner does one 80 percent conventional mortgage and one 10 percent second mortgage underlying the first and thus completely does away with the need for PMI. As home prices go up, the PMI providers lose their previously booked business, as insurance is no longer needed. If prices go down, they lose their older booked business to refinancings. Heads you lose, tails you lose—not exactly the best business model for an industry.

And it gets worse. The PMI industry has gotten into a fierce battle with Fannie Mae and Freddie Mac, who wanted to eliminate the need for extra insurance coverage on mortgages with 90 and 95 percent loan-to-value ratios. The PMI providers responded by forming a lobbying group called FM Watch to lobby Congress about Fannie Mae and Freddie Mac's egregious lobbying that was initiated to protect their borrowing advantages and subsidies. Lobbyists watching lobbyists—dogs and cats living together—what is the world coming to? It would be funny if it were not so sad. We have witnessed many times companies lobbying Washington for subsidies, but this is the first case of two industries achieving mutual deterrence in their lobbying efforts in order to protect each other's time at the trough. When you sit in the dentist's chair and he puts those pliers in your mouth, and you reach over and grab the dentist's nose, we say you have reached dental equilibrium—you don't hurt me and I won't hurt you. It seems the PMI industry and Fannie Mae and Freddie Mac have reached dental equilibrium.

Not only is the PMI industry at greatest risk if there is a downturn in home prices, they are also the most critical element in the entire home mortgage business. What if the PMI provider's guarantee turns out not to be worth the paper it is written on? This will have enormous ramifications not only for the mortgage investing business but for homebuyers because it will carry over into mortgage rates. If the PMI industry gets in trouble, mortgage investors get in trouble, liquidity evaporates for home mortgages, rates shoot up, qualifying formulas for new homebuyers tighten, and home prices decline. So, the feedback to the marketplace from a minor price decline might indeed be a more major decline.

Fannie Mae and Freddie Mac—A Potential $3 Trillion Problem?

The greatest damage a PMI industry problem could do is to its old nemeses, namely, Fannie Mae and Freddie Mac. The only joy the PMI providers will get in failing is knowing that they have mortally wounded their archenemies with the blast of their final implosion. These two monoliths of the residential mortgage business have become the backbone of the entire market. If a contagion reaches inside the comfortable offices of Fannie Mae and Freddie Mac, there is no pessimistic scenario I can describe that will adequately depict the ensuing disaster.

Many who examine these two very large companies are initially swayed into complacency by their sheer size, their AAA ratings, and their incredible record of reported earnings growth over the years. However, one does not really understand these institutions until one pulls back the curtain and finds that a rather impotent old man is actually pulling the levers. I will walk you through an incredible story of power and ambition, but at the end, I'm afraid all that will remain behind the curtain will be man's common afflictions of avarice and greed.

The only other warning I will give before I begin this wild ride through the financial condition of Fannie Mae and Freddie Mac is to remind readers that the numbers get very big. To appreciate the potential calamity involved you are reminded that $1 trillion is the same amount as one million bags of $1,000,000 each. We know, it is still incomprehensible, but at least we tried. Now fasten your seat belts!

According to their annual reports, in a home mortgage market of $5.7 trillion, one government agency, Ginnie Mae, and two quasi agencies, Fannie Mae and Freddie Mac (the FMs for short), hold on their balance sheets or guarantee $3.7 trillion in residential mortgages. We told you the numbers were going to get big! To put it in perspective, this is getting close to the entire U.S. government debt of $6.3 trillion, which has taken 290 million people over 225 years to assemble. The FMs' debt was forecasted to pass the total U.S. debt balance soon, but unfortunately, our government went from a trillion dollar surplus position to a trillion dollar deficit position, so we guess they will lope along together. To show you how recent a problem this is, and to demonstrate the dramatic growth that these quasi agencies have experienced, the FMs had on their books or guaranteed only $132 billion of mortgages as recently as 1982.

In John Cassidy's excellent article in *The New Yorker* titled "The Next Crash," he writes that William Poole, the president of the Federal Reserve Bank of St. Louis, recently warned that the sheer size of Fannie Mae and Freddie Mac could create a "massive problem in the credit markets." What would happen, Poole asked, if the market value of the bonds that they use to finance themselves fell sharply, because investors grew concerned about the financial soundness of Fannie Mae or Freddie Mac? "I do not know, and neither does anyone else," he said.

Lots of Leverage but No Risk!

Figure 9.6 shows that the FMs accomplished this dominant size with very little real equity. Counting all their mortgage debt holdings and guarantees, Freddie Mac is levered 71 times its equity of $17.6 billion and Fannie Mae is levered 116 times its equity of $15 billion. The Basel

Accord of 1988 maintains that international banks have to maintain maximum leverage ratios of 12 to 1 on their loan portfolios and 24 to 1 on their residential mortgage portfolios. Unfortunately, the FMs do not need to comply with Basel. These FMs are incredibly large institutions, two of the largest financial institutions in the world, which also happen to have, possibly, the highest leverage in the world.

This leverage act is the circus equivalent of the largest animal, say the elephant, performing the riskiest maneuver in the circus, say walking the tightrope. Regardless of his skill, you would be advised not to sit underneath the high-wire act, regardless of how entertaining you might find it.

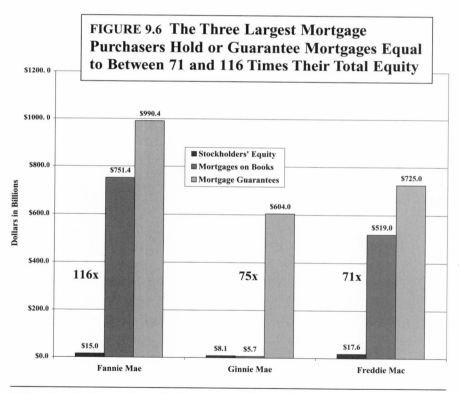

FIGURE 9.6 **The Three Largest Mortgage Purchasers Hold or Guarantee Mortgages Equal to Between 71 and 116 Times Their Total Equity**

Source: Annual and quarterly reports for the Federal National Mortgage Association, or Fannie Mae, the Government National Mortgage Association, or Ginnie Mae, and the Federal Home Loan Mortgage Corporation, or Freddie Mac

Similarly, Fannie Mae and Freddie Mac have provided a wonderful service to homeowners over the last 20 years. They have provided enormous liquidity to the home mortgage market, making home purchase available to many. Some 67 percent of families in America now own their homes, an incredible statistic that is extremely beneficial to the general economy and the stability of the nation.

Lately, we would argue, these institutions have begun to lose their way. The elephant may be beginning to teeter, and I for one will not just look the other way. Figures 9.7 and 9.8 show that both Fannie Mae and Freddie Mac have enjoyed tremendous earnings growth and share price appreciation. The story does not stop there. There is a much darker tale about how this growth was accomplished and what these institutions might be hiding from the public.

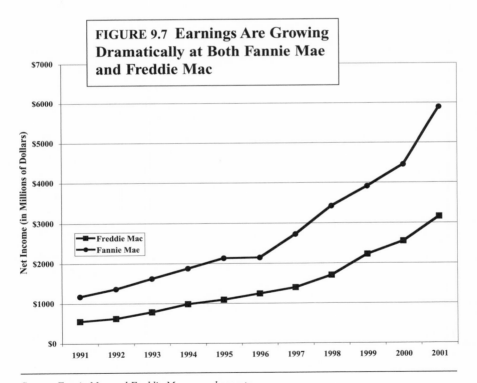

FIGURE 9.7 Earnings Are Growing Dramatically at Both Fannie Mae and Freddie Mac

Source: Fannie Mae and Freddie Mac annual reports

In my opinion, companies as leveraged as these two behemoths, narrowly focused in just one business and one asset class, do not deserve a triple-A credit rating. Their rating reflects neither their financial performance nor their financial condition, but something much more basic: their corporate charters. Both were "privatized" in the 1970s and 1980s when they were spun off from the federal government. Rather than becoming fully private enterprises, they maintained some very important advantages of being quasi-public agencies of the federal government: Their charter says that they are exempt from registering their securities with and disclosing financial information to the Securities and Exchange Commission (SEC). This alone makes it very difficult to do a thorough investigation as there are no 10Ks or 10Qs to review. They

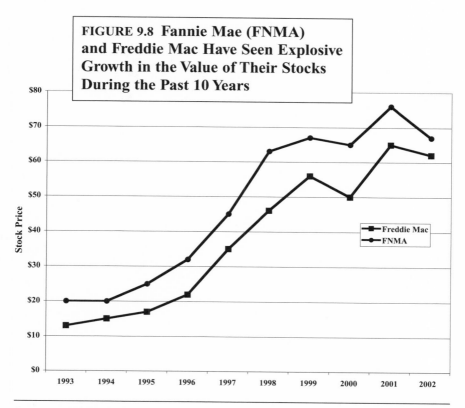

FIGURE 9.8 Fannie Mae (FNMA) and Freddie Mac Have Seen Explosive Growth in the Value of Their Stocks During the Past 10 Years

Source: New York Stock Exchange

are also exempt from state and local taxes. The President gets to appoint five members of their boards and the Treasury gets to approve their debt issuance. But the big daddy of perks is more implied than clearly stated. The marketplace clearly believes that the federal government stands behind and guarantees all Fannie Mae and Freddie Mac debt and commitments. It is because of this implied U.S. government guarantee that the FMs have triple-A ratings and can borrow at almost the same rate as the federal government.

This low borrowing cost is an enormous subsidy provided by American taxpayers, and is estimated at $6.5 billion per year by the Congressional Budget Office. If this subsidy just went toward lower mortgage rates, no one would be the worse.

The problems with giving your largest industry participants a government guarantee is multifaceted. First, it puts other private competitors at an enormous disadvantage. This means that the FMs can fund their mortgage costs at such low government guaranteed rates that they can buy business at yields that make no sense for private businesses. You would expect industry consolidation in the hands of the FMs and that is just what has happened, with approximately 90 percent of all conventional mortgages being held or guaranteed by the FMs. Not only is such consolidation bad for any industry, but also the implied government guarantee of the FMs allows them to do many noneconomic things to win business.

Second, the government guarantee allows the FMs to be much more aggressively financially, and not pay any financial cost for their irresponsible actions in terms of higher borrowing costs. Every day companies make decisions as to how aggressive they will be in how they finance their business, but they know there will be a cost: the more inexpensive debt they use in their capital structure relative to expensive equity, the higher yield they will have to pay debt investors to purchase that debt. For the FMs, there is no such trade-off between increased risk and financing costs. No matter how badly they run their business, their financing costs do not change, thanks to the federal government's implied guarantee.

Now it also turns out that the FMs are very much like private companies in one very important aspect: They grant their managers and executives enormous stock option plans. So, like good private businessmen they are motivated to improve earnings and increase their stock prices. But unlike a normal management team, and because of their government guarantee, they can do some fairly risky things to try to create shareholder value. The only thing I can think of that is worse than having a government agency as a competitor is to have a for-profit business as a competitor that has a government guarantee.

The prime example of how the FMs increase profitability by increasing risk is by increasing leverage. Increased leverage always increases the rate at which earnings grow, but it also increases the rate at which earnings decline in bad times and raises breakevens. The extra debt should increase the firm's borrowing costs, but thanks to the federal guarantee, this doesn't happen for the FMs. When the FMs increased debt leverage in their business, they did it solely to enhance the value of their employee stock options. They didn't care a hoot that they were endangering the entire mortgage market of the United States. Running a government business for private gain reminds me of Ross Perot's attempt to privatize the post office in which all he asked for in return was 10 percent of the savings.

How they increased leverage is equally disturbing. First, it turns out that the FMs were so big and growing so fast that the only way they could grow faster was to move into new markets. Individual conventional mortgages have a maximum dollar amount to qualify to be bought by an FM. The FMs got their limit indexed to home price appreciation so it now stands at close to $325,000 per mortgage. Indexing a lending constraint to escalating and artificially high home prices is no constraint at all, sort of like a fox at a henhouse constraint—the more hens that are eaten, the more hours per week the fox is allowed to guard the henhouse. This escalating constraint on home borrowing amounts is likely to have been a major contributor to the recent runaway in home prices.

Second, when the FMs ran out of conventional mortgages to buy, they started going after sub-prime mortgages. These are multifamily and second mortgages or lower credit first mortgages that carry a great deal more risk than conventional mortgages. But, no worries, mate—the FMs' borrowing rates will not change thanks to the government guarantees.

Finally, and probably most offensively, to add assets as fast as possible, the FMs didn't go out and find new homebuyers that wanted to secure a mortgage—they simply went out in the secondary market and bought a bunch of mortgages off the street. No productive activity here, just a chance to pop earnings by living off their low government guaranteed borrowing rate. Buying secondary assets on the street is in direct violation of the FMs' charters that call for them to supply mortgage money to homebuyers.

Oh, I forgot: Where Fannie Mae and Freddie Mac used to book only about 25 percent of their total commitments and just guarantee the rest for others to hold, now they book approximately 60 percent, leaving few mortgages for anyone else to hold. The reason is simple: If they take the increased risks of interest rate risk, early principal repayment risk, and counterparty risk inherent in holding a mortgage rather than just guaranteeing it, their profit margins increase nearly fourfold. Oh, yes, and once more their borrowing costs do not change to reflect the riskier strategy because of their government guarantee.

And remember the catfight the FMs had with the PMI providers about no longer needing PMI on 90 and 95 percent mortgages? The real reason is that the FMs wanted to cut out the expense of paying PMI on these loans, which would increase the risk of the portfolio, but, well, you know, no worries because of their government guarantee.

The Next Great Disaster

I am at a loss when I try to compare the FMs to anything I have seen previously. Given their lack of regulation, the enormous utilization of derivatives in their business, and the general complexity of their financial statements, they share characteristics of other troubled companies of late. I challenge anybody to read their annual reports and tell me within $3 billion how much real cash flow either of them makes each year.

If things turn badly, this situation might have the potential to be similar to the S&L collapse of the 1980s. Like the S&Ls, they hold only home mortgages, an asset that nobody has ever figured out a way to make riskless or to fix maturity on without a government guarantee. Also like the S&Ls they enjoy an enormous government guarantee and subsidy in their borrowing costs. Finally, they both suffered through stressful times, the S&Ls during the high interest rates of the eighties and the

FMs in their self-imposed prison of trying to provide constantly increasing profits for Wall Street, their stock price, and their management options. If home prices decline, that just might be the straw that breaks the FMs backs.

An examination of Fannie Mae's most recent annual and quarterly reports raises serious questions as to what the effects of all this risk-taking has been on the cash flow available to shareholders. I cannot emphasize enough how convoluted Fannie Mae's financial reports are, so I raise these concerns only as questions, to which Fannie Mae's management will hopefully have some good answers. Like other companies facing dire circumstances, Fannie Mae has recently tried to get investors to focus on new definitions of financial performance, such as operating income figures instead of GAAP net income numbers and a pro-forma net worth rather than GAAP-defined shareholders' equity. I am reminded of the magician who asks us to focus all our attention on his right hand as he takes our wallet with his left hand.

It appears as if the wheels might finally be coming off the Fannie Mae bus. Combined over the last two quarters ending September 30, 2002, Fannie Mae has taken off-income statement hits to their retained earnings totaling $26 billion. The explanation they give for these charges has to do with how they account for their callable debt and their derivatives. While incomprehensible, the effect on the company's shareholders' equity account is unmistakable. During the last six months book equity has declined from $20.7 billion to $14.9 billion! This is beyond remarkable for a company that has experienced double-digit growth in earnings for the last 20 years and is claiming record earnings performance for this six-month period.

In addition, Fannie Mae's annual cash flow is actually running more like $15 billion per year as compared to the $5.9 billion they report as net income on their 2001 income statement. This is because for each of the last two years Fannie Mae has reported an additional off-income statement cash source of $10 to $11 billion per year flowing through their cash flow statement. While completely untaxed, these funds go fairly much unaccounted for by people examining the company.

So, in summary, over the last two years, Fannie Mae seems to have earned $28 billion in after-tax cash flow, paid $2.5 billion in dividends, but had their book equity remain flat. What did they do with the money?

I first thought that they had accomplished major share repurchases. I checked and they had repurchased $2.0 billion worth of shares during this period, but their total shares outstanding barely changed. In essence, for every share they repurchased, they issued an option share to management. Too bad Fannie Mae is not subject to regulation by the Securities and Exchange Commission.

Finally, who does Fannie Mae and Freddie Mac report to? You better know it in advance because it is not a name you would ever guess: the Office of Federal Housing Enterprise Oversight, known affectionately as OFHEO. I don't know what is worse, the cumbersome title or the acronym, which is difficult to pronounce and to remember. In the most classic case of the tail wagging the dog, or Brer Rabbit begging not to be thrown into the briar patch, in 1991, Congress, in its wisdom, subjected the FMs to the scrutiny and regulation of OFHEO. I guess if you cannot go unregulated, a brand-new group of regulators of your choosing is the next best thing. It is interesting that in 1999, when OFHEO was trying to get an increase in its funding, the FMs' lobbyists worked hard to put a cap on it. I guess the only thing better than an unknown, small regulatory agency looking over your shoulder is an unknown, small, poorly financed regulatory agency pretending to look over your shoulder.

The biggest problem driving the apparently irrational behavior of the FMs' managements is the implied guarantee of the federal government for its liabilities. We have seen that this guarantee not only drives the FMs to do riskier and riskier things to increase profits, but also has had an overreaching impact on the entire mortgage industry. Competitors, as well as suppliers to the FMs, have to take greater and greater business risk, at smaller and smaller margins if they wish to compete or do business with the FMs. It is generally impossible to have a stable market when one of the competitors has no incentive to control its risk-taking.

Even without the government guarantee issue, industries with long asset lives such as the airlines, the banks, the insurance business, and the mortgage business have long had a reputation for behavior that we will characterize as "irrational competitiveness." It is the nature of industries with very long assets and liabilities, and very small probabilities of tragic events, that the participants will compete on price until they no longer adequately allow for all hard-to-define risks in their pricing. In the short term, business flows to the competitor who ignores the long-term risks and therefore prices his services too low. In a competitive market, there is great pressure on the other participants to match this mis-pricing. If they do not, they will not have any customers. Of course, we have seen the result of such cyclic behavior. Profits and retained earnings are driven to such a low level that when the tragic scenario occurs, many of the market participants do not have adequate equity cushions to withstand them. Some view such industry shakeouts as healthy, and compared to government bailouts, we would have to agree. But it seems as if the dislocations to customers, employees, and taxpayers might be avoided if we could do a better job identifying the industries subject to this of type behavior and isolate its effects. The mortgage industry is exactly such a long-lived asset industry. Irrational competitors will drive rational players out of the market, will crush profit margins in good times, and will not survive the bad times ahead.

In maybe the worst example ever of throwing fuel on a fire, Congress in its wisdom in 1997 decided to liberalize the treatment of capital gains on homeowners' primary residences. Where previously, a couple could exempt up to $500,000 in capital gains on a sale of their home once in their lifetime, under the new provisions they can utilize a $500,000 capital gains tax exemption every two years! This tax benefit was added at a time when houses were increasing in price at a record pace, Fannie Mae and Freddie Mac were already benefiting from their implied government guarantees, and homeowners already had a significant tax break in the form of mortgage interest deductibility. The net result was to make housing the most favorable asset class of all in terms of tax treatment and to further drive up prices in what was an already overheated market.

The most disturbing part of this story is the same conclusion I reached in 1999, which led me to work on the presidential primary in New Hampshire the next year: Money from big corporations has much too much influence over our government's legislators and regulators. It is why I believe meaningful Campaign Finance Reform is so desperately needed in this country. As long as Fannie Mae and Freddie Mac can contribute millions of dollars to Congressional campaigns, legislators will be worrying more about the health of the FMs' management teams' port-folios than the health of the nation's mortgage market. It is a travesty of our form of governance that this problem has to explode before it can be disarmed. It is a joke that someone like me has to write about such a mess in order to clean it up. This is the job of our legislators and regulators who haven fallen down and cannot get up. When our country's history is updated, I hope all government employees who have fed at this unethical and infected trough are held in the same regard by historians as Benedict Arnold.

Summary of Chapter 9

- Under a worse-case scenario, it will not just be overly leveraged homeowners who will be in trouble if there is a decline in housing prices.
- Commercial banks hold $1.5 trillion in home mortgages, have aggregate book equity of less than $500 billion, and are experiencing greater and greater rates of default on their mortgage portfolios.
- Seventy percent of the private mortgage insurance (PMI) market is composed of five small firms who have guaranteed $530 billion of highly leveraged property with total book equity of only $11 billion.
- If the smaller PMI providers begin to default, this spells real trouble for Fannie Mae and Freddie Mac as they depend on such insurance for many of their most leveraged mortgage holdings.
- Fannie Mae and Freddie Mac are two of the largest financial institutions in the world, holding or guaranteeing mortgages worth approximately $3 trillion and having leverage of 116 and 71 times equity, respectively.
- Fannie Mae and Freddie Mac have an implied government guarantee that makes them immune to the costs normally associated with riskier and riskier behavior, including utilizing higher leverage, encouraging faster asset growth on their balance sheet, and holding riskier sub-prime mortgages.
- Fannie Mae and Freddie Mac are driven to increase earnings to feed an ever-increasing stock price to the benefit of shareholders and option-holding management teams.

- Fannie Mae and Freddie Mac are exempt from filing or reporting to the SEC.
- The entire mortgage industry is dancing faster and faster in a world of escalating prices, increased leverage, historically low interest rates, and overly aggressive lending terms. The music is about to stop!

10

Summary and Conclusion

We have examined the U.S. housing market in rather excruciating detail. What have we learned?

We have seen that no matter how you measure them, home prices in the United States look awfully high. Nationwide, the average home has appreciated in price eightfold over the last 34 years. Even after adjusting for inflation, home prices are up almost 70 percent during the period. Some of this increase can be explained by the building of larger homes, but there is still a very large increase that remains unexplained. This unexplained appreciation is even larger than you might think if you subtract out the recent value of the tax deductions inherent in a home purchase, which have declined since 1980.

In the last three years, the economy has weakened, unemployment is up, the stock market is down, and yet housing prices are up. Housing prices relative to household incomes are up, even knowing that household incomes have increased substantially due to a greater number of married women working. Housing prices are stable or up in many metropolitan areas of our country where rents are down. This anomaly cannot last forever. The recent interest rate decline has clearly contributed to the higher home prices, but you do have to wonder if the rate decline will be permanent.

There is incredible debt leverage throughout the housing market. Consumers hold record amounts of debt in aggregate and are entering into more and more low-money-down mortgages. Mortgage foreclosures and personal bankruptcies are at record highs. And this is occurring during a period of rising home prices and relatively good economic prosperity.

We have seen that real economic markets can have some irrational participants and still act rationally in assigning prices and allocating resources. We also have seen that the efficiency of a real economic market should obviate the extreme swings of bubbles and crashes. How can we then claim that the housing market is acting irrationally in setting its home prices and is a bubble economy waiting to burst? Simple: The housing market is not a true economic "market." There are very few lenders who provide most of the capital, in essence determining the prices paid for homes.

As we move further and further away from an ideal market, we increase the likelihood of bubbles and crashes. A crash is very likely in the near future in housing because interest rates will either go higher, causing lower bank qualifying amounts and home prices to decline, or will head lower, signaling a very weak economy, also causing home prices to decline. Recent highly leveraged home purchases and refinancings have left many homeowners swimming in debt and adopting the risky profile of a pure option holder, essentially playing with other people's money. Banks are not motivated to control risk as they pass through most of the mortgages they originate to other purchasers, earning very big profits in their mortgage businesses. Self-policing in the mortgage business has collapsed as buyers are not price-sensitive; banks do not hold the mortgage assets on their books; appraisers are not completely independent; regulation and government oversight is very lax; and the two largest mortgage holders, Fannie Mae and Freddie Mac, have implicit government guarantees making them the polar opposite of risk averse.

Participants in the mortgage business have been lulled into a false sense of security. The fact that home prices have increased every year for the last 40 years has everyone involved overly complacent when it comes to addressing downside price risk. Homeowners seem to think if they only own one home and they fix their mortgage payments, they are not subject to any risk. Buying bricks and mortar must have some soothing appeal to homeowners who recently got their clocks cleaned in the virtual Internet crash. Fixed rate borrowers have not thought much about what might happen to them if rates tick back up, and adjustable rate borrowers have not thought much at all! Lenders think they are adequately hedged against interest rate movements and mortgage prepayments, but other than some geographic diversification, really have no answer as to how to handle or manage default risk in their mortgage portfolios.

When we look at the problem from a regional perspective, we find that 40 of the metropolitan areas that we examined had home price appreciations greater than 35 percent over the last five years. Only lonely San Jose had a decline in its average home prices in the last 12 months, and that was solely because they had appreciated so much over the last decade with the boom in Silicon Valley. It appears that many of the cities with the highest home prices five years ago experienced the greatest price appreciation over the ensuing five years. Sort of the rich getting richer, or maybe the rich getting dumber! Many cities' average homes are selling far in excess of the recommended maximum ratio of three times average household income. In the last two years, home prices across the country have tripled the rate of growth in incomes. This book presented an innovative method of comparing your city's home prices to local apartment building prices to see if home prices are relatively overvalued and not reacting quickly enough to falling rental prices and a weakening economy.

We examined five prior crashes in recent memory to see if there were similarities to today's overheated housing market. We found that in many of those crashes, bank leverage played an important role as it decreased the principal's true economic commitment to the transaction and left pricing decisions up to a distant, and rather unaffected, bureaucrat. Typically, government got involved, not as a reasoned regulator, but as a guarantor of last resort or as a biased participant in the proceedings. We saw that common sense was displaced by the fear that participants might miss the next profitable opportunity, sort of a self-imposed Ponzi scheme. No one made you do it; you decided to do it to yourself! Finally, in many of these examples of crashes, the economic activity, while vigorous, did not pass the basic textbook rules as to what is needed to make a true "market." Without these basic market assumptions being fulfilled, the transactions were susceptible to enormous price swings, bubbles, and eventual crashes.

How will it all begin? Well, depending on where you live, it may have already started. San Jose is beginning a decline, San Francisco is leveling off, pricier homes are not selling in Portland, and Honolulu continues its retraction from heights not seen since wealthy, but land- and golf course–poor, Japanese disembarked on their shores in the late eighties. Our economy continues to stumble along, with the only bright note being money taken out of homes in refinancings being spent on consumption goods. If rates increase, housing should go down; but if rates decrease, housing should also go down. Heads you lose, tails you lose! If mortgage interest deductibility is threatened in Congress, desperate to balance a budget severely in deficit, or if lenders become less aggressive in their mortgage terms, prices may also go down. If prices decline it may prevent homeowners from selling, thus significantly reducing labor mobility and harming the fragile economy further. Typically, housing price downturns lag economic downturns as homeowners are slow to reduce their asking prices. Any argument about housing being scarce has not taken into full account the aging of the baby boomers who already own homes and the significant number of homeowners who are over the age of 65 and will be transferring ownership of their homes in the future.

Under a worse-case scenario, it is not just homeowners who will suffer. The entire mortgage industry, including commercial banks, PMI providers, and Fannie Mae and Freddie Mac, are all highly leveraged and prone to doing more and more risky things to increase their profitability. While the weakest link in the food chain appears to be the smaller PMI providers, it is Fannie Mae and Freddie Mac that present the greatest worry. That is because they sit on or guarantee $3 trillion of home mortgages, and with their implied government guarantee, seem to keep doing riskier and riskier things each day. Let us hope our government ignores the campaign donations it is receiving from these two mortgage gorillas and does what we hired them to do—regulate their borrowing and investing activity. If we fail in this task, in my opinion we could potentially be looking at an economic disaster that would surpass the trillion-dollar S&L debacle of the late eighties. The ramifications could be so severe that it is not unrealistic to think that such an event could trigger a worldwide depression as the credibility of all banks and investment companies would be threatened.

You might think that it is fun to write a book such as this. I admit some of the economic analysis has been fun, but the conclusions are anything but. A family member asked me if I was concerned that I might cause a real estate crash by writing such a book. I explained that the crash was not the problem—the policies that allowed the bubble to be created in the first place were the real problem. If I didn't expose these systemic problems and risks inherent in the housing market, then prices might continue their upward glide until the fall was even larger and more catastrophic. My greatest hope in writing this book is that people will listen to the logic of my argument, prices will settle gently without anyone getting hurt too badly, and we have the good sense as a people and a government to fix the problems endemic to our housing and mortgage industries. After this furious dance, when the music stops, I hope my readers will be near a comforting chair, which may be unlikely if they took my advice and sold their homes!

On a somewhat more optimistic note, let us now take a look at what each of you can do right now to minimize any negative impact a housing crash may have on you and yours. The next section focuses on 10 principal areas and offers many practical suggestions as to how you can survive the coming crash.

PART II

AND WHAT YOU CAN DO ABOUT IT

Following is a list of 10 actions that you can take to protect your most valued investment if you believe home prices have a real risk of declining in the near future. While I recognize that some of these actions are much more difficult to implement than others, I thought it would be helpful to lay out the entire spectrum and let readers decide which actions are most appropriate for them. Readers who wish to explore options involving publicly traded securities should consult a registered broker dealer for advice as I make no recommendation here as to the values of such securities and neither give nor imply any transaction or valuation advice.

Action Item 1:

Decrease Your Exposure to Residential Real Estate

You might conclude that the only thing you can do to avoid losing money if home prices decline in the future is to sell your home immediately. While this might make sense for some true believers, such drastic action surely cannot be the only recourse available to reduce exposure to a possible decline in housing prices. It is with this in mind that I list a number of alternatives, some obviously more difficult to enact than others.

There are significantly more barriers to selling residential real estate than stocks. It takes a great deal more time, there is a great deal more paperwork and administrative work to be done, and there are many more emotional ties to your home than to your stock portfolio. How do you tell your teenage daughter she has to give up her bedroom or move to a new city and say goodbye to her friends? Therefore, we will spend a great deal of time talking about less stressful alternatives rather than the option of selling your home outright.

First, if you are not currently a homeowner, but are looking to buy, maybe it is time to change your mindset. Our analysis shows that maybe you do not have to be in such a rush to buy a home. Many young couples have a feeling that if they do not buy right now, they will be priced out of the market forever. They envision a world in which they are perpetual renters, never fully enjoying the comforts their parents had in owning their own home or the associated good feelings of family, friendship, and warmth associated with home ownership. If they extrapolate historical housing growth rates into the future, they realize that if they do not buy now they will never be able to afford a home.

Housing price increases every year for the last 35 years has fueled this belief. As prices really started to accelerate over the last couple of years, the feelings that this was your last chance to buy probably grew. In addition, there is a misconception frequently stated in the press that somehow houses are growing more scarce. Fueled by real estate brokers interested in increasing home prices, this theory says that available land has been exhausted for home building and that a great immigrant wave will create enormous pent-up demand.

Anybody who thinks that available land is exhausted has never traveled around our country by automobile. Maybe a house in Manhattan, New York, is beyond your means, but probably not one in Manhattan, Kansas. Anybody who argues that all the great towns have been taken, like Los Angeles, San Francisco, San Diego, and Seattle, doesn't know about potentially great cities in the future that are just starting to be recognized. Who is to say that Jacksonville, Nashville, or Charlotte will not be dynamic cultural centers 15 years from now? Larger cities, such as Los Angeles and Seattle, have not found a way to deal with their traffic, crime, and pollution and as such might have less appeal 15 years from now.

The idea that a resource like housing will run out and become scarce is an old concept in economics. Famous philosophers have argued for decades as to whether we were exhausting our natural resources. Generally speaking, after taking into account monetary inflation, prices are lower today for most commodities than they were in 1970. It is difficult for resource scarcity to explain price increases in housing because, by definition, a price increase must mean that people did not recognize the scarcity effect before the increase. Anybody explaining beachfront property increases by arguing that it is scarce or limited would also have to explain why people 10 years ago were so clueless as to believe that coastlines were of infinite length. You cannot have it both ways.

When they are confronted with a price history for an asset like the straight-up growth housing has experienced the last 35 years, most people assume it will trend higher and higher. They forget the future has at least four or five alternative states. Housing prices may go higher, they may flatten out, they may decline gradually, they may collapse, or they may go up and down with no real sense of direction. If I am right, the probabilities are that the housing market has a lot more potential downside from these price heights than additional upside potential.

While I doubt many existing homeowners will rush to sell their houses having read this book, I will consider the book a great success if it breaks the mindset of potential homebuyers that prices will always be heading higher so they had better hurry if they want to purchase a home. If new homebuyers read this book and it convinces them to delay their purchase, I will be very pleased. Hopefully, prices will soften as predicted and these loyal readers will be able to make their purchases at much more affordable prices and under much more agreeable terms.

For those of you considering purchasing a home, try to exercise some personal constraint in deciding what price to pay for your new home. Please do not depend on bankers, realtors, mortgage brokers, and appraisers, none of whom are disinterested observers, to help you decide how much to spend on your new home. Make a reasoned decision as to the amount of mortgage payment you can afford each month without becoming a slave to your house. Maybe it would be best to make this decision before you look at homes. Once you see a house you like it will be hard not to accept an unusually high mortgage payment to move in. Please do not allow the bank qualifying formula to determine the amount you are going to spend. If you spend 20 to 30 percent less than the total amount you qualify for you should feel extremely comfortable with your repayment ability, and you should probably reward yourself for having incredible self-constraint. A good rule of thumb is not to pay more than three times your family's total household income. And unlike during the boom times, do not make the mistake of buying a new home before the sale on the old home closes. The last thing you want to be is the unexpected owner of two homes when the market heads south. Finally, it is probably not a good time to think about upgrading to a bigger, more expensive home.

You should be very concerned if you are purchasing a home in those metropolitan areas that we identified as being most likely to be overvalued. If you are buying in a town we did not include in our survey, then do some homework to find out median home prices and median household incomes. You can easily divide to see if the town has an income multiple greater than three, which would put it in the riskier category. Even if you exercise price constraint in your own eventual purchase, your new home may be caught up in a neighborhood or citywide price decline.

Exercising such price constraint is easier to talk about than to actually do. Not only is it psychologically hard to adhere to spending limits and avoid the siren call of a big beautiful house with a pool, but spending less than you qualify for is very difficult when everybody else in the world is spending as much, or more, than they qualify for. The fact that home prices are overvalued, and that this is ascribable to overaggressive lending and borrowing, means that if you spend less than you qualify for you will probably be looking at homes that do not quite measure up to your standards. Your day will come, however, when your properly priced home survives a housing downturn with only a modest price decline, while the $500,000 wanna-be down the street quickly becomes a $300,000 fixer-upper. Remember, the key to being a good investor, and this applies to home real estate investors as well, is patience. Most poor investment decisions are made when the buyer feels he is under some sort of time pressure to act. It is up to the sellers, and in the case of homes, their agents, to create this false sense of urgency. Please, do not get caught up in it.

If you are already a homeowner, you have a number of options available to you to minimize your exposure to home real estate, but they all have significant transaction costs associated with them. If you are unwilling to relocate, or accomplish a similar major lifestyle change, and you want to be hedged against the risk of a housing price downturn, maybe you should explore purchasing a put option from your financial adviser. If your financial adviser can recommend a stock or index that trades closely with the housing stocks, then buying puts on this index or group of stocks should allow you to hedge some of your home's exposure to housing price declines. In effect, if you do not sell your home and a housing price decline occurs, you will lose money on your house, but make it up on your put position. I will caution you about option hedging. It can get expensive over time, it can be difficult to figure out exactly how big a put position you should take to effectively hedge your total house exposure, and even if you get the ratio right there is no guarantee that the hedge you create will move dollar for dollar with your home's price. Worst case, your home could decline in a local housing crash, but your put hedge may not appreciate at all if the national housing stocks it is based on do not suffer commensurately. I have two pieces of advice: Be careful, and get the advice of a financial adviser very familiar with options, futures, and hedging. More on this later, under Action Item 4.

You can, of course, always move boldly and take the more direct course—just sell your house. If you do, you have a number of alternatives. You can rent temporarily in hopes that you time the price collapse correctly, or you can buy something more modest. If you rent, do not be afraid to splurge on the monthly rent as it is only temporary, and I do not want your family to suffer. If your monthly after-tax payments (because you will be losing the tax deductibility of owning) are $1000 more each month for 18 months, this is a small price to pay for saving $100,000 to $200,000. You should get a fairly good deal in renting, as rents have not kept up with housing price increases recently in many metropolitan areas. The *Wall Street Journal* on August 5, 2002, reported that a number of homeowners, convinced that the housing market is a bubble about to pop, are deciding to cash out, and stay out. Instead of buying new homes, they are renting until prices fall back.

Moving into something that is lower in price will decrease your exposure to any future price declines and should allow you to pocket some mad money in case you have other bad events to weather ahead. Ideally, not only will the price be lower, but you will utilize much less debt and therefore have much lower mortgage payments. Any monthly savings, again, can go to a rainy-day fund. Make a game of it with the kids. They will get a real kick out of their two-year stay in the two-bedroom cabin, and you will save enough to pay for their Harvard education. As an extra bonus, you and the missus might just remember how much fun you had when you were starting out and that fun in life is not a function of the number of closets or bathrooms you have in your house.

I told you that this would not be an easy issue to deal with, especially if you believe our analysis. People forget in good times how illiquid real estate investments are and how difficult it is to adjust your exposure. If people did not sell their technology stocks at the peak because they thought it was too much of a hassle, then they probably will not want to get involved in this hassle. But, if you do, and you act to protect your net worth, you will appreciate the bounty for years to come. In 10 years the world will be made up of those who cashed in on the technology bubble at its peak and sold their homes when housing prices were still high, and those who took the ride up and back down again with nothing to show for it.

Action Item 2:

Move from a High-Priced Area to a Lower-Priced Area

You could move from a currently highly overvalued metropolitan area to an area that is less overvalued. The exhibits we created in Chapter 6 can be very helpful in determining which areas of the country are the most overvalued. If you happen to live in one of these relatively pricey areas, you can help yourself tremendously by moving to a less expensive area.

You will reap a one-time windfall, as you will be able to buy much more house for much less money. I would recommend downsizing, or maintaining your current size house, even though you can afford much more square footage in the new town, as there is no assurance that the new town's prices will not decline also. You can also accomplish the same effect by staying in your home city, but moving to a less expensive neighborhood.

If the entire country's home prices are overvalued, then your new home will decline in price, but the decline would just be much less than in your old town. This is what is meant by relative overvaluation. They may both decrease in price, but the loftier price neighborhood should fall farther. This thinking is very similar to P/Es in the stock market. The higher the P/E, typically the greater the stock will fall in a recession. This is because most of the power behind a big P/E is due to growth that usually suffers in a down economy. Similarly, most of the overinflated value behind a high housing P/E home will be attacked if housing prices fall.

You may face a significant tax bill. An individual can exclude as much as $250,000 of any gain from taxation, while a married couple filing jointly can exclude $500,000. If a couple sells a primary residence for $1.2 million that they had purchased previously for $500,000, they would exclude $500,000 of the $700,000 gain from taxes; thus only $200,000 would be subject to taxes at a maximum possible capital gains rate of 20 percent. Total taxes due in this example would be a maximum of $40,000.

Depending on what you do with your monetary windfall, this may become a permanent move. If we are wrong about the relative price declines you may be prevented from buying a house in your old neighborhood or city. This should not be the case with a significant price decline, but you should prepare for all eventualities. This means that you should take this move very seriously as if it were going to be permanent. You might find that a move away from the traffic-congested city to a friendlier smaller town is just what the family needed. The stress associated with big city living can get to be a drag on everyone in the family. If you plan it right, your savings may increase dramatically as watching your son's Little League games in a small town can be a lot less expensive than dinner at a four-star French restaurant in the big city.

Action Item 3:

Manage Your Debt Leverage Better

Housing would not be a risky investment except for the extreme amount of leverage we place on our homes. There are very few businesses or asset classes that can be leveraged as much as a family home. The reason is fairly straightforward. Banks extend enormous amounts of money to homeowners because they know that homeowners will do anything before they let the bank foreclose and take the family home. It is hard to think of an asset that a person holds more dearly than his home. Possibly a wedding ring, but judging by the sheer number of wedding rings you see in pawnshops, probably not.

Smart financial borrowers in the business world, if they have to pledge collateral, always try to pledge an asset that is extraneous, that they can walk away from if necessary, something that is not essential to run the business. Homeowners do just the opposite. They pledge the most important asset they and their family possess. This gives the bank great comfort when extending credit secured by a first mortgage, and it explains why lenders like to turn unsecured credit card debt into secured home equity loans through refinancings or second mortgages.

But sometimes, events happen beyond the family's control that make the continuing timely payment of the mortgage impossible. Defaults and foreclosures do happen to people just like you and me. Therefore, let us talk a bit about how to manage the amount of debt on your home properly.

First, if you are looking to buy a home, the best way to avoid taking too much debt is not to pay an exorbitant price. You may have paid too much relative to other similar homes in the neighborhood, in which case you might be able to service the debt, but you might have problems repaying it when you sell. Or you might have paid more than your budget allows. Even if you get a good deal on a house, if its price is outside of your budget, you may get into serious trouble with your mortgage payments.

To prevent overpaying, make good use of the rules of thumb on valuation you found in this book, paying particular attention to the city-by-city analysis. To avoid spending more than your budget allows, try to stay within a budget of not paying a home price of more than 3 times your household's total annual income. With conventional levels of debt financing this should give you adequate funds to service your mortgage and have a life outside of your home.

Besides paying too much for your home the second way you can get into trouble with debt leverage is to have too much of it. Radio and television commercials are always advertising mortgage deals with 10 percent down, 5 percent down, or no money down. There are seminars offered where you can learn to buy real estate with no money down. The commercial shows rather despicable people living in a mansion as if to say that if people like that could do it you should be able to also. I made the mistake of entering the words "mortgage refinancing" into my search engine on my computer and got 112,000 hits. Clearly, there are plenty of people out there who want to encourage you to borrow more than you probably should.

In the latest sign we are reaching the end of the party, there are now ads for interest-only loans. These are a new kind of mortgage in which your total payment goes to pay interest only, there is no principal being paid back. If you owe $250,000 today on your house, you would make monthly payments of say, $1250 each month for 30 years and still owe $250,000 on the house. Such financing is reminiscent of Donald Trump's mortgage deals in which he was dependent on future price appreciation to repay the loan. It also reminds me of some shady LBOs in which the arranger tried to give zero-coupon paper out as consideration to shareholders. When a market gets so stretched that people or companies cannot even pay interest and/or principal on a loan, it is good sign that the market is peaking and it is time to get out.

So buying a home takes a great deal of self-control. If you are not careful, a lender will see you for what you are to them, an unencumbered wage earner. The way he makes money is by finding such species and loading as much debt as possible on them. You will be in a very sorry state if you depend on your banker or mortgage broker to advise you as to the proper level of debt. With today's rate environment we have seen that the amount that you qualify for will quickly become difficult to handle if rates tick back up in the near future.

I believe an individual or couple should not borrow more than 80 percent of the value of a home. Although higher amounts of leverage with lower down payments are available in the market, we do not believe these transactions have your best interests at heart. You have to assume that the price you pay for your home will be, at least, a fair price, that there are no dramatically undervalued homes on the market. If this is the case, then putting more than 80 percent debt on your home reduces your flexibility in the future and limits your options. You should be prepared, in any market, for a price decline of at least 20 percent, without causing your home to go underwater, that is, to have the mortgage balance exceed the market value of the home.

Now what if you are an existing homeowner who finds himself with too much debt, say more than 80 percent of the current conservative value of your home using some reasonable downward adjusted price based on how overvalued your particular city might be? If you really want to do yourself a favor and plan for a potential housing crash, you will do one of two things.

First, you could begin a concerted and organized effort to pay down each month more than your scheduled mortgage payment. Most mortgages allow early prepayment, with any additional amounts paid in excess of the scheduled monthly mortgage payment being subtracted from your principal balance. We would recommend laying out a family budget and then making a family commitment to a higher monthly payment. If you just wait until the end of the month to see how much extra cash you have laying around, we doubt you will ever make real progress in reducing your debt. I know I wouldn't.

You could also make a lump sum payment on your mortgage to bring its debt down to a level you are comfortable with. Where will you find the proceeds for such a lump sum payment? Sources of funds are all around you. You can sell the family's fourth car. You can tell your son how you used to walk to school, two miles each way, and then sell his car. You could take a boarder in and have him pay some rent to cover part of the mortgage. (More on this option later.) You could sell some stocks or bonds. You could spend some of that tuition money you have been saving for your kids. I have news for you: The colleges are just going to take it all anyway. You could call your rich grandmamma and see if she wants to be your real estate partner. (Better to owe her some interest than the bank; hopefully if you are late with a payment she will be more forgiving and not put her family out in the street.) If you quit thinking of mortgage money as free money and see it for what it is—a threat to your family's well-being and your livelihood—you will find the cash to do what is necessary.

The second alternative gives you more flexibility, but requires more self-discipline. Rather than taking a lump sum of money or increasing your monthly payments to pay down your mortgage debt early, you could start saving in a separate account to be used for one purpose only, in case there is trouble with the family's mortgage debt. Finding lump-sum sources now and putting them in such a lock box makes sense, as the car may be not worth as much in a recession and you may not be such a good credit risk to grandmamma in the future if you have lost your job or divorced her favorite daughter. This approach takes enormous discipline as there will be lots of reasons every month, especially if times get tough, to raid this account for other purposes.

There are three advantages to this approach. First, if you use the money to repay your mortgage debt, it is gone. You don't control it, your banker does. You can't get it back. Under the lock-box solution, you have full control of the funds. If absolutely necessary, you could use the funds elsewhere. You will have much more negotiating strength if you ever have to face a possible foreclosure. Second, if the housing market really tanks, you may want to walk away from the house. If you were going to do this it would be better for there to be more, not less, debt on the home. If you are going to go up in flames, it might as well be a heck of a bonfire. Third, if you repay your mortgage early, you lose the tax deductions associated with the interest deductibility. The flip side of this argument is you probably do not want to invest the lock-box money in any risky assets, so I doubt you will find a better yield for the funds, even including the tax benefits, than prepaying your mortgage.

Proper management of debt exposure is not limited just to managing the amount of debt. It is also important to manage interest rate risk. If you are a first-time buyer, I would recommend always locking in whatever interest rate you are quoted for the documentation period while you wait for the mortgage to close. This is one of the only free options left in the world, as you can always walk away and do your business elsewhere if there is a precipitous rate decline during the time it takes to close. Most of my comments, however, have to do with how existing homeowners can better manage their interest rate exposure.

If you are an ARM borrower, refinance into fixed rate debt immediately! You are at the greatest risk of getting in trouble if there is a housing crash. As we saw earlier, one cause of housing prices crashing would be a sudden increase in interest rates. New homebuyers would not be extended as much financing under such a rate scenario, so they could not afford to pay at the level of current high prices. As an ARM borrower you would suffer a double whammy. While your home's price was evaporating, your mortgage payments would be increasing rather quickly. You are right that if you locked in today you would be missing out if rates declined further, but do you really see 10-year Treasuries heading much below 4 percent? If they do, I believe the economy will fall into a deflationary spiral so your mortgage payment will be the least of your worries.

Non-ARM homeowners should also seriously consider refinancing at these low rates. If current rates are more than one full point higher than your current mortgage rate, it might make sense to refinance. It depends on whether you have prepayment penalties attached to your current mortgage and whether bankers continue to offer aggressive low-fee loans. Remember, if you are planning on moving anytime soon, it probably will not pay to refinance as you will not enjoy the lower payments long enough to make up for the up-front fees you will have to pay.

Now when we say refinance, we mean a reasonable refinancing, not reflecting what the term has come to mean in popular parlance today. Specifically, we would not recommend a refinancing package that puts more than 80 percent debt on your home relative to its true inherent value, again adjusting for any current market overvaluation. Also, all moneys borrowed should go to repaying your existing mortgage. The only exception is funding renovation work on the house if you are 100 percent certain you will be able to recoup the added investment in the house in an increased sales price. This should limit you considerably because there are very few home projects that pass this test. Installing a new hot water heater, probably; building a new deck or pool, probably not!

Under no conditions are you allowed to take money out of the house and make purchases or pay down other debt balances. Remember like Hollywood, the money must stay up on the screen! While it makes good economic sense to turn nondeductible credit card debt into deductible mortgage debt, the danger is that it leaves you with the powder dry on zero-balance credit cards. I know of few people who can withstand that temptation. Part of the debt problem that families are suffering from today is that they converted their 30-day credit card debt into 30-year mortgage debt through a refinancing. Their debt is now more permanent, is not required to be repaid, and they gave up a security interest in their house to holders of what was their credit card debt. You can argue that tax advantages made them do it, but sometimes you have to say no to stupid tax advantages.

It may be the case that to satisfy the conservative advice above you have to write a check to accomplish the refinancing. You may have too much debt on your home currently, so to get debt levels down you may have to put in additional equity capital. Now, I know, you will be the laughing stock of the neighborhood. At the country club, people will gawk as you walk by and say, "There goes the only guy on earth that refinanced his mortgage and had to put more money in rather than take money out." Two points: First, the reason for refinancing is to take advantage of lower rates, not to increase your debt loads or finance other toys. Second, you will have the last laugh if housing prices crash as the club members will have to wait in line to ask you for a personal loan to help them make their monthly mortgage payment.

Action Item 4:

Hedge Your Exposure to Residential Real Estate

For many readers, the thought of actually selling their home and either downsizing or moving to a less overvalued town will always remain academic exercises. The family is just too attached to your home and there are already too many accumulated memories and experiences that have occurred in the house. While not insisting that you sell, please remember how strongly you feel about your house. It will help you gain the courage to make other difficult adjustments necessary to ensure you never lose your home. Following are things you can do to hedge, or minimize your overall exposure to a potential housing price crash, short of selling your home and renting.

First, you should examine what other real estate holdings you own. If you cannot part with your primary residence, maybe it is a good time to sell your vacation home if you own one. Clearly, it is not a good time to buy a second home, especially if you get the down payment moneys by putting a second mortgage on your existing home. If we are right, you can always buy a bigger second home for the same money in a few years time. Unfortunately, *USA Today* on November 12, 2002, reported that research by the National Association of Realtors showed that 13 percent of purchases of second homes involved some use of first home equity in the last three years, versus 8 percent previously. This is the definition of doubling down.

There is no good reason to own more than one home with prices at these levels. If you own any investment property that you are renting out, seriously consider selling it now. Even if you own your own business and office space, we would recommend doing some sort of sale/lease back in which you continue to occupy the space but do not have any of the price risk associated with the space. While office or commercial space is outside the scope of this book, under a worse-case scenario in a housing crash, we would expect the general economy to suffer. It is reasonable to assume that some of the price decline contagion would find its way into the office market.

Next, it is probably time to take a good hard look at your investment and retirement portfolios. Most Americans have more equity invested in their homes than they do in their stock portfolios, yet I have never heard of a broker suggesting that you reduce your exposure to housing in your stock portfolio. It is only natural, given the theory of diversification, that if you have half your total net worth in your house, you probably do not need to be holding any housing stocks in your investment or retirement portfolios. Even when you buy indexed mutual funds that hold the market portfolio, you are adding a significant amount of housing risk to your total risk profile.

Peter Englund, Min Hwang, and John Quigley published a research paper in *The Journal of Real Estate Finance and Economics* in 2002 which showed that a properly structured portfolio that minimizes risk, including your residence, should have between 0 and 50 percent invested in residential real estate. They conclude that many households could hedge their overexposure to real estate and garner an extra return, without exposing themselves to any additional risk.

It is fairly easy to identify the obvious companies that track fairly well with housing. The big quasi-agency stocks, the big mortgage originators, the PMI providers, and even some of the banks that have substantial residential real estate exposure would all be good candidates. You should talk to a professional investment adviser if you want to do a thorough job of sanitizing your portfolio of housing risk, as there are many stocks that trade in tandem with the housing cycle but are not necessarily housing stocks: furniture manufacturers, for example, or moving companies.

As long as you are addressing general housing risk in your portfolio, you might also want to address geographic risk in your portfolio. If your home is hit with a significant price decline, it probably will hit the rest of your neighborhood and geographic region as well. To the extent that it might set off a regional economic slowdown, it probably does not make sense to have your portfolio heavily weighted with local companies. It might make sense to lighten up on companies that are doing an unusually large percentage of their business in the same town where you live. In this case, familiarity really might breed contempt.

Even if you eliminate all housing exposure in your investment and retirement portfolios, you still have a very big overall exposure to housing prices just by the very nature of remaining a homeowner. There is no easy or clean fix to this problem. Any solution is less than perfect, but we should discuss them.

With other assets, especially very liquid and frequently rated and priced securities like stocks and bonds, there are sophisticated ways of eliminating your exposure of ownership without actually selling. For example, if you wanted to eliminate your exposure on a stock you own, say, IBM, but for some reason did not want to sell, you could easily buy a put on IBM, such that your net position was neutral. Any loss on the stock would be covered by a commensurate profit on the put. Puts are nothing more than bets that assets will go down in price. While risky if held by themselves, when held with the underlying asset, IBM stock in this example, the total net holding eliminates almost all risk and exposure of ownership.

If there were such a thing as a put market that sold specific puts on your house at 207 W. Beall Avenue, then we could recommend your buying such a put to hedge your exposure to any price declines on your house. Unless you have a neighbor who is bullish on housing prices and wants to write such a put option for you, you probably will have to do the next best thing.

Since you cannot buy a put on the exact value of your house, you should try to find a put that sells on a liquid asset like a stock that trades very closely and positively with housing prices. We have seen that the big quasi agencies are such animals, and there are puts available on them. Any mortgage originator should do nicely also.

The risk in such a transaction is that there is no guarantee that the put value will trade exactly with your house value. By definition, these are imperfect hedges. Under many future states, you will have been better off for having hedged your exposure, but there is always the chance that the hedge does not work as expected and you end up worse off. There are events that could affect one of the quasi agencies directly, such as legislative changes, which may not have a price impact on your home. In such cases the hedge will not work as anticipated. Always consult a professional financial adviser, and in this case, one who is very familiar with hedging and options trading.

Robert Shiller and Allan Weiss wrote a paper in 1999 for *The Journal of Real Estate Finance and Economics* in which they argue for the creation of home equity insurance. Not PMI insurance, which protects investors from default, but rather insurance for homeowners that would protect them from declines in the market values of their homes. The insurance company would act as a retailer and distributor of larger short positions in traditional hedging vehicles in the futures and options market. The authors also suggest that there would be real demand for an insurance product that was tied to a decline in home prices and triggered by specified life events, such as moving to take a new job in another city. While theoretically correct, no insurance company to date has taken them up on their proposal.

A final method for minimizing or hedging your exposure to a market downturn in home prices may not be so obvious to financial types. You can always bring a boarder into your home to rent a room to. The rent he or she pays can go toward the mortgage payments or can be used to accelerate the pay down of the mortgage debt. If your monthly mortgage commitment is 30 percent lower as a result of renting out a basement apartment, then you have effectively lowered your exposure to housing market movements. It will take a much more serious price decline or family problem to get you in trouble with your bank.

Action Item 5:

Plan Now in Case of a Major Transition Event

Given how dearly families value their homes, it usually takes a fairly serious event to cause a homeowner to default on his mortgage payments and risk foreclosure. Nobody wishes to lose his or her family's home. While we all suffer cash flow problems of one sort or another at some time of our lives, minor cash shortfalls are usually not sufficient reason to risk foreclosure. More significant unexpected events like a job loss, a divorce, or a medical emergency are needed before a family surrenders to money pressures and forfeits its home.

The most common reason for mortgage default is a job loss in the family. While most job losses occur unexpectedly, there are things that you can do today to manage the risk of a possible job loss in the future. The problem is complicated today by the fact that in close to 70 percent of homes in America both parents work. Normally, you would think of this as providing a cushion, since one adult could lose his or her job and the other could keep working and pay the bills.

In the modern world of home mortgage financing, unfortunately, there is no such thing as a cushion. Remember, banks take both spouses' incomes into account when figuring out how much mortgage debt money they will extend. They do not apply any discount to the sum of both wage earners' salaries. It is as if one big wage earner were applying for a mortgage. Therefore, the lenders make no allowance for either adult losing his or her job. Because they put so much debt on the couple, rather than having a cushion, the couple faces greater risk than the single borrower. If either of them suffers a job loss, the mortgage is endangered.

Clearly, regardless of what fields the parents have chosen to work in, there is a higher probability of either one losing his or her job than a single parent losing his or her job. Simplistically, there is double the probability of either of two parents losing his or her job as compared to a single parent. The incredible amount of bank borrowing has made home ownership by a couple riskier than it is by a single parent. This seems to violate one of the principles of marriage, namely, that there is safety in numbers or that two incomes are better than one. When it comes to highly leveraged home mortgages, no man is an island, but many may wish to be. It is also not a mistake that the lenders hold couples joint and severable for all debt liabilities. They know that if one party loses his or her job, it is best for the bank to be able to go after the sole remaining breadwinner.

Since there is very little you can do once you suffer a job loss, other than falling on your knees and appealing to your boss's sense of compassion, it makes sense to discuss what things can be done today to prepare for such an unlikely event as a job loss in the future. Here, we are talking about job dismissals and firings. We assume that no one tied to large mortgage payments would ever walk out on his job without having another firmly lined up, regardless of what name the boss called you. And, if you do wish to change jobs, make sure you have something in writing from your new boss before you leave your current job. There are bosses who wait until you are jobless before negotiating the details of your pay package at your new job, and sometimes they introduce new terms that can be deal killers. I believe big mortgage debt does more to create cooperative and friendly work environments than if we put Valium in the office water cooler. People under the constant threat of mortgage foreclosure cannot afford to be anything but model citizens around the office.

What can be done today to plan smartly for a potential firing in the future? First, as the employees of Enron unfortunately found out first-hand, it probably does not make a lot of sense to have a great deal of your own company's stock in your investment or retirement portfolios. One event that can cause employee dismissals is a corporate bankruptcy, and it can cause them in droves. The last thing you want on the same day you find out you no longer have a job is to realize that your investment and retirement portfolios have taken a beating because your prior employer's stock was a primary investment. Again, this is an example of where even though you are most familiar with your own employer's prospects, and think you understand the risks, in the name of simple diversity you need to divest your holdings of your own company's stock. You will recognize the lack of diversity in your total portfolio if you assign a market value to yourself based on your current wages, and realize that this human capital market value will temporarily decline if you are dismissed. Just as you don't need any more exposure to housing stocks if you are a homeowner, you certainly don't need any more exposure in stock ownership to the company that employs you. Also, make sure that your investment portfolios are very well diversified and fairly conservatively invested as you already have enough concentrated risk in your own human capital and home ownership investments.

The most important thing you can do to plan for a possible, though hopefully very unlikely, dismissal is to negotiate a severance contract today. I have never negotiated such a contract, but I have always been disappointed at what was offered from the jobs that I held. It makes sense to have this contract negotiated now, as the severance payments will be crucial after a dismissal in helping you stay current on your mortgage payments. It also makes sense to negotiate it today as your boss will be much more generous now, while you are currently an outstanding performer, than on the day of your dismissal when he has a much lower appreciation of your work skills.

Different couples have different arrangements as to how they deal with their finances. I do not want to pretend that I know anything about how couples manage their affairs, as I am a lifetime bachelor with no on-the-job training. Regardless of whether you and your wife handle financial matters informally or very formally, it probably makes sense to have a sit-down and discuss what will happen if either of you loses his or her job. At least a verbal arrangement should be agreed to as to whether any additional moneys needed for the mortgage will come from commingled funds, or whether the fired party has some responsibility to reach outside the family and find additional sources of capital. Like I said, I don't understand how couples do these things, so I will leave it at that.

In addition to job loss there are other traumatic life events that can make it difficult to remain current on your mortgage payments. Divorce has to be considered a major threat to stable home ownership, especially given the mortgage lenders' propensity to lend to two salaries as if they are one. Although few couples have signed prenuptial agreements as to how assets will be divided in divorce, we think it is time to put into writing exactly what will happen to the house in case of divorce. Not only is it important to know that you have adequately planned for your children's well-being in providing a home and shelter for them, it is also good to know that you have thought through a contingency plan that prevents the loss of your home.

In divorce, it is not just a question of who gets the house and kids. Because one person's salary is probably not going to be sufficient to pay the mortgage, you must decide now how child support payments will be directed to ensure the home is safe. If you cannot come up with a satisfactory solution as to payment support, maybe it is time to think about different alternatives. It would be very difficult if at the same time you were seeking a divorce the housing market collapsed. Maybe we will have a new generation of kids, not raised in broken families, but worse, raised by a couple who wanted to separate but couldn't find a buyer for their home. We will call them the unfortunate children of "unbroken" homes.

If you find these discussions with your mate terribly difficult and uncomfortable, ask yourself why the banks do not insist on your having them before they lend you hundreds of thousands of dollars to buy a home. Maybe they don't want to listen to them either. Sometimes unpleasant topics must be addressed, sort of like telling your children about drugs. And remember, when a mortgage banker offers you more money to buy a house than you can afford to pay back—Just Say No!

The final major life event that can threaten your home is an unplanned medical emergency. Given the cost of medical care today it is unlikely that any family could survive a major medical scare without adequate insurance, so I will address how to handle this occurrence in Action Item 7, on the importance of maintaining adequate insurance. Suffice it to say that all family members should get regular and thorough checkups as it is always better, medically and financially speaking, to catch ill health early and then adopt a resurgent plan to better health.

Action Item 6:

Examine Other Contingency Plans

Anybody who has his or her favorite and largest asset owned with 80 to 99 percent secured debt financing ought to be thinking about contingency plans. If you wait for bad events to occur, they may turn out to have disastrous consequences. I know that the Boy Scouts' oath includes always being prepared, but here I would like to emphasize that we all plan ahead. If you want a more carefree lifestyle that involves less forward planning, just sell the house. You will have a lot less to worry about. But be sure you discuss it with your spouse first or you may have a great deal to worry about.

Under the adage that money solves all problems, the most important thing you can do to plan for an uncertain future is to have a substantial rainy-day fund. Like the U.S. Congress, the difficult part in holding such unallocated funds is in not spending them. I would think you would want to have funds equal to at least 25 percent of the value of your home invested very conservatively. Because it is the nature of surprises that you don't expect them, holding a general fund for all types of occurrences makes sense. You most likely will not expect the shock that threatens your home ownership. This is a truism. If you expected it, you would have planned for it and it wouldn't be considered a surprise. No sensible person leverages himself or herself with so much debt without holding something back in reserve.

When I was working on Wall Street we did an LBO for a Fortune 500 company in which the numbers worked, cash flow covered interest expense, but just barely. The CEO wasn't stupid. He held back one of the company's gold mines in Nevada and did not use that cash flow to pay debt. It got confusing when I tried to explain the deal to my Wall Street associates. Concerned about the amount of debt on the company, they asked if we knew what we were doing, to which I always replied, "Don't worry, we have a gold mine." To which they would say, "Great, what is it?" And then I would say, "No, really, it's a gold mine!" And then, they would say . . . Often this would go on for hours, à la Abbott and Costello stuck on first base.

In addition to holding cash in reserve it makes sense to get control of your other debt exposures. Pay down your credit cards and tear up most of them. Pay off your car and boat loans. Convince your children that state universities are one of the last bargains remaining and try to minimize student loans. Be very careful about giving your children credit cards as this is a license for parental bailouts. I am convinced the reason the banks like to give credit cards out on campus is so they can eventually get into the parents' wallets through threats of destroying their children's credit rating for the rest of their young lives.

If you don't happen to have 25 percent of your home's value lying about, consider borrowing it. A friend or relative will be much more likely to lend you money today when you are fully employed, not divorced, and not sick, then later under different circumstances. Take the money and put it in a very safe investment, not long government bonds as these do very poorly when rates increase, just the state of the world that might do the most damage to your home's value.

You might also approach a bank about arranging a revolving credit agreement. This is a line of borrowing that is contractually available to you if you need it in the future, but which does not have to be drawn down now. It has the advantage of not costing you much today, as all you have to pay is a small fee to assure its availability. If you did a conventional loan you would lose on the difference in yield spread between what interest rate the bank charges you and the yield you can garner on a safe cashlike investment with the funds.

The most important thing in negotiating the revolver is to make sure there will not be any additional conditions at drawdown that might prevent its use. A provision that you must be fully employed at drawdown or that you be current on all other debt payments would be counterproductive in building the safety net that we are trying to construct here. We don't need a line of credit that is only good in good times; we need to be able to access funds in bad times as well.

I'm beginning to feel like a life insurance agent with all this discussion about planning for life's bad events. It is about to get worse. You might find my next suggestion completely vulgar and offensive. Another way to plan for life's uncertainties, if you can not raise additional capital today, is to plan on reducing your financial commitments in the future. Namely, it might make sense to explore what alternatives you have in selling personal assets, boats, cars, antiques, into a weaker economy, knowing full well that prices then will be lower than what you could achieve today.

And now for the maximum in unpleasantness, you should consider what you would have to do if it became necessary to bring a boarder into your home. You should investigate if your local town's codes and ordinances would allow multiple family living. You might want to build out a separate bachelor pad over the garage, with kitchen, bath, and bedroom. If things don't turn negative, you could always use it as an office and guesthouse. A tenant on your property can bring a sense of security to your spouse and children and can help tremendously in helping you make mortgage payments if things get tight. You might just find yourself a new best friend!

Action Item 7:

Maintain Adequate Insurance

If in purchasing real estate there are three rules to follow, then when buying insurance there is but one. Never insure a loss you can afford to take. What does it mean? It means that insurance is not inexpensive. Insurance companies know a great deal about probabilities and they price the policies to cover their risk and overhead costs and allow for a healthy profit margin. In other words, buying insurance is like betting against the house in Las Vegas. The odds are against you.

Therefore, you should only buy insurance when you cannot afford to take the loss associated with the insured event. The most egregious violation of this rule that I witnessed was in a Radio Shack store. The woman in line in front of me purchased an alarm clock for $12 and then purchased an optional three-year warranty for $19.95. $20 of insurance on a $12 item makes little sense, but the woman should have known not to buy any insurance as she could have afforded the $12 loss if the alarm clock stopped working. The fact that a manufacturer is willing to sell you additional warranties indicates that he believes, and he should know, that the unit probably will not need the warranty.

If you owned six or seven homes and were a multimillionaire you might consider going without home insurance as you could probably get by if you lost one of the homes. Conversely, if you own but one home, it is very important you have adequate insurance should anything happen. Fire, theft, earthquake, flood, etc. should all be insured against to protect your home. In addition your home policy should cover any personal liability event occurring on your property, such as someone slipping on the front steps.

But in order to protect your home in the upcoming uncertain housing market, you need to insure more than just your house. We have seen that traumatic events are what drive families into home foreclosure. Unexpected medical expenses are one area in which insurance can definitely help.

Forty-four million Americans today have no medical insurance. Originally a problem of the poor, this problem is slowly infecting the middle class. Many people in the middle class are either unemployed or between jobs and have let their insurance lapse. Many others have taken on more entrepreneurial careers and being self-employed they have not adequately planned their medical insurance needs. Homeowners and their spouses without medical insurance are asking for problems with their mortgage payments.

Even those who carry medical insurance may not have adequate medical insurance. Hospital costs have become so expensive that everyone ought to review his or her policy to see that coverage is sufficient. Additionally, many policies do not adequately cover long-term disabilities, just the type of occurrence that could threaten a home mortgage.

Similarly, we have seen that many mortgages depend on two people's incomes to adequately service the debt. It would only be reasonable if both earners had adequate life insurance. If they can afford it, it would be good if the benefit payment was sufficient to pay down the entire mortgage. In a home of a one-parent wage earner it would be nice not to have to worry about house payments.

I don't think there are any insurance companies that write policies against divorce or job loss. This is unfortunate. These two events will get more families into mortgage trouble than any others. A previously negotiated divorce settlement involving a cash paydown of the mortgage would be helpful. There is no substitute for good planning with regard to a possible job loss.

Action Item 8:

Investigate Bankruptcy Protections Now

Although no one wants to discuss the possibility of bankruptcy, it pays to do your homework in advance. Bankruptcy laws change from one state to the next, so anything said here should be modified to reflect your local laws. Also, I am not a bankruptcy expert, nor do I pretend to be one, so please consider this discussion as an initial primer and refer to a bankruptcy expert or attorney in your area for more detailed and professional advice.

First, it goes without saying that if there is any alternative to bankruptcy, it will most likely be more favorable. Bankruptcies stay on your credit record for up to 10 years and will severely affect your ability to borrow in the future. But given the amount of mortgage and consumer debt on many families in our country, a number will find themselves with no other practical alternative. It is best to be knowledgeable about the basic procedures, even if you do not foresee utilizing them in the near future. Remember, it is unforeseen events like job losses, divorce, and medical problems that cause most people to default on their home mortgages.

Bankruptcy is a legal method of eliminating debt from people that are overleveraged and suffering a cash shortfall. If, after paying your monthly expenses for necessities, you do not have enough funds to pay your creditors, then you may be eligible for bankruptcy. You must live, do business, or own property in the United States, and you cannot have been granted Chapter 7 relief in the last six years to qualify. You also cannot "substantially abuse" the bankruptcy process and qualify for relief.

What is Chapter 7 bankruptcy? This is the most common form of personal bankruptcy and only individuals can qualify. Under this arrangement, a court-appointed trustee collects your assets, sells them for cash, and makes distributions to creditors. You can keep assets that are exempt either under Federal law or the law of your home state. Under this bankruptcy plan, typically all debts are removed from the debtor. The exceptions are state and local taxes, some student loans, and debts that were induced by fraud. Debtors usually are allowed to keep their personal property including their household goods. A homeowner is able to keep his home under Chapter 7, but only if he or she does not have more equity in the home than each state's homestead exemption. For example, Illinois currently limits home equity values to a maximum of $7500 or else the homeowner will have to forfeit the property.

And what is Chapter 13 bankruptcy? In Chapter 13, a debtor comes up with a three- to five-year plan that pays all or a significant amount of his debts off from his or her future earnings. Again, this plan is only available for individuals and not for corporations or businesses. The individual must have a demonstrated source of future income, and there must be a definite amount of disposable income budgeted to pay the debts off in a timely manner.

People choose Chapter 13 over Chapter 7 for various reasons, even though it does not completely free them of their debt obligations. Some people have unusually large state and local taxes due, which are not dischargeable in a Chapter 7 reorganization. Also, homeowners who are having difficulty keeping current on their mortgage payments may choose to file a Chapter 13 plan to help them keep the original mortgage agreement in place. Payments due under the mortgage and other credit agreements can be deferred under a reasonable plan, but the agreements remain in effect and the home is not lost as it might be under a straight Chapter 7 filing. If you are already facing foreclosure, the mortgage lender's legal recourse may only be temporarily stalled under Chapter 7. Also under Chapter 7, co-signors of your debt can be stuck with the full amount of the loan unless they file also. Under Chapter 13, your co-signors are protected unless you fail to repay the debts in full over time. Under either plan, creditors are prevented from taking legal action against you once you have filed your bankruptcy claim. To file under Chapter 13, your total debt must be less than $1 million, and your secured debt, such as car and mortgage debt, cannot exceed $750,000.

Some states exempt people's homes from bankruptcy proceedings, but most just have exemption limits. If the equity in your home exceeds the dollar maximum limit, the bankruptcy court in Chapter 7 may grab your house and sell it to pay other creditors. This is a big advantage of Chapter 13 over Chapter 7 for homeowners. If you file under Chapter

13, and agree to a plan to get current on your home mortgage and other debts, then you cannot be foreclosed or lose your house as long as you are current with your plan. The court can also allow a longer period of time to pay off a debt that has been accelerated due to default. In Chapter 13 it would be possible to buy time to make payments, making up the missed payments out of your income through the repayment plan. This avoids the requisite selling of your home to facilitate debt repayment. Chapter 7 filers, in many states, have no such protection.

A Chapter 7 bankruptcy can take three to four months, but relief from creditors is immediate upon filing. A Chapter 13 bankruptcy can take three to five years to completely pay off your debts. In a Chapter 7 proceeding, you have no obligation to pay interest and principal on old unsecured debts you are trying to discharge in the bankruptcy, but you should stay current on debts secured by real assets like your house and your car that you are trying to preserve. If you stay current on your secured debts like your mortgage, you should be able to keep your home through bankruptcy, so long as you do not have too much equity in the home. You should contact your mortgage holding institution and reaffirm the mortgage debt with them directly. This reaffirmation agreement can then be filed with and be approved by the court.

You cannot be discriminated against by an employer for having filed for bankruptcy. You also cannot fraudulently run up your credit cards prior to filing as this falls under the abuse provisions of the code and these obligations will not be forgiven in the proceeding. It is a felony to try to hide assets from the court in a bankruptcy and will, most likely, result in fines and the denial of your bankruptcy petition.

If we are right about the downward direction of home prices in the future, there will be a large number of people who will have more mortgage debt than the market value of their home. This means that their home equity will be negative. In such a circumstance, it probably makes little sense to reaffirm their mortgage debt with the courts or try to save the home. It will probably make more sense to have the court sell the house and distribute any proceeds to the creditors.

If this discussion has sounded at all complex, please realize we have summarized less than 1 percent of the bankruptcy law applicable to homeowners. Because of the general complexity of the bankruptcy law, and because federal law allows individual states to set exemption limits and develop their own property laws, we cannot emphasize enough the need to talk to a bankruptcy expert in properly planning for the future. Nothing we have said here should be regarded as expert advice and no one should rely on anything presented here as fact or a fair representation of the facts. How is that for a legal disclaimer?

Action Item 9:
Become More Civically Involved

It would be nice if we were all entirely self-sufficient. If we could solve all of our own problems without the assistance of others the world would be a much simpler place, albeit probably a somewhat lonelier place. Unfortunately, this is not the case. Many of our most worrisome problems require the cooperation of our neighbors, our local residents, and our fellow Americans. The difficulty of organizing cooperative efforts might explain why it is exactly these types of problems that occupy so much of our time. If they were easy to solve, they would have been solved already.

When cooperative effort is required among civilized peoples it usually takes the form of government. Not only is government organized to allow cooperative effort, but only government has the necessary powers of policing and enforcement to punish uncooperative types who try to cheat the system.

Regardless of how well you manage your personal financial affairs, things can happen in Washington that directly affect your ability to repay your mortgage as well as the value of your home. It is essential that you become actively involved in your government if you are to protect the value of your investments. Voting is important, but it is not enough. On important issues you have to write letters, send emails, and telephone your senators, congressmen, even the president. In a world of big money and powerful special interests infecting Washington, the only chance the average citizen has is by making his or her voice heard loudly and often.

What issues currently being negotiated in Washington should be important to homeowners? Well, one of the most pressing is the banks' attempt at changing our personal bankruptcy laws. With very little input from average Americans, the banks have gotten very close to reducing the bankruptcy rate by making it more difficult to claim. Anti-abortion types prevented its passage last time, but we cannot be certain that they will always be there. This is a classic example of good citizenship because you must act now to protect your rights in the future, even though you face no eminent threat of bankruptcy. It just happens to be the right thing to do.

If we are to return the mortgage industry to firm footing, we need to be sure regulations are in place to prevent individual participants from destroying the system. Specifically, we would favor legislation that required that new homebuyers have a cash down payment at least equal to 10 percent of the purchase price. This down payment could be a cash gift from relatives or friends, but could not be borrowed funds under a second mortgage or borrowed on an unsecured basis. Such regulation, while offensive to true free market types, would assure that people paid some attention to the prices they were paying for homes and put some constraint on the dangerous leverage being employed.

With regard to leverage, we would put an end to the practice of second mortgages where the total debt-to-loan ratio exceeds 80 percent. Such second mortgages or equity loans are extremely risky and are used to circumvent the requirement for private mortgage insurance. If the mortgage lending market gets into trouble, it will be these second mortgages and equity home loans that lead the way.

I would favor legislation that reigns in the residential appraiser community. True independent appraisers are needed, with no ties, actual or implied, with the realtor, mortgage banking, or commercial banking industries. With regard to appraisals, more work should be done to extend the appraisal beyond what a similar home down the street sold for recently. Per square foot comparisons can be made across cities and historically, over time, so that buyers are not throwing good money into a bubble economy. Some comparison to apartment building prices and potential rental income would also be appropriate.

The entire private mortgage insurance industry needs review. We should put a maximum on the ratio of property they can guarantee relative to their book equity. Something like 15 or 20 to 1 seems appropriate, which means there should be an immediate and mandatory consolidation of the smaller, more leveraged players in the industry. Waiting for a price downturn and then trying to put Humpty-Dumpty back together again seems like an awfully shortsighted way to regulate an industry. If we allow this industry to fail, the ramifications to mortgage lenders, and especially Fannie Mae and Freddie Mac, will be enormous. For individual homeowners it will mean a drying up of credit for home purchases, tightening of terms in the mortgage market in general, and possibly catastrophic price declines in housing.

In my opinion, Fannie Mae and Freddie Mac pose the biggest hurdles to real legislative reform. They are two of the largest and most powerful financial institutions in the world, and they will greet any attempt to reduce the risk in the mortgage system as a direct attack on their potential for profitability. Because their managers live on stock options, which depend on increasing stock prices, which demand improving earnings, any attack on their ability to increase earnings in the future will be met with the stiffest of resistance.

What is unfortunate is that these companies are no longer doing smart things to increase earnings in the future. No one would quibble with a management that is creatively thinking of new ways to provide much needed service to its customers and is being rewarded with steadily increasing earnings. Unfortunately, this is not what Fannie Mae and Freddie Mac are up to. They are taking on greater and greater risk to add additional leverage and push to their earnings stream. With steadily increasing debt leverage, where now Fannie Mae holds or guarantees mortgages equal to 116 times its book equity, it is time to recapitalize these firms and bring their leverage down to reasonable levels, say, 40 to one.

These companies should be forced to abide by their charters and only be allowed to buy new home mortgages. They should be prevented from purchasing mortgages in the secondary market, solely in an attempt to buy yield. Both FMs should be prevented from holding second mortgages or home equity loans and should be forced to divest their subprime businesses and assets.

Most importantly, the FMs must be completely privatized. Their implied government guarantee must be revoked. Because they are so large that a government bailout is almost a certainty, they should be forced to split up into more manageably sized companies, say $250 billion of assets and guarantees, to start. This might give private enterprise a chance to compete in this business and bring some sense of reasonableness to the pricing structure in the industry. Finally, Fannie Mae and Freddie Mac must be prevented from using their market muscle and government contacts to coerce other market participants such as PMI providers or privately owned competitors.

Liberals and libertarians will have two very different solutions to these problems. Libertarians will insist that much of the market distortion will disappear if we just get rid of the implied government guarantees the quasi agencies enjoy. The liberals will want to enact regulation that is more thorough and make sure regulatory bodies are doing the job they were hired for. I can sympathize with both sides. I do believe that the government guarantee is the single biggest problem in the entire industry. But I also believe that companies should not be allowed to grow to such a size that they dominate their markets, hurt fair competition, and make it impossible for them to fail gracefully. If we made our super-sized companies split up, there would be little lost to economies of scale and all markets would be fairer and more competitive.

I assume your reaction to these suggestions is that they look theoretically interesting, but enacting them is not your job. Well, it turns out that it is your job. It is each citizen's job. If we do not get involved in our government's business, our government will surely get involved in our business. Ideally, we elected representatives who are supposed to deal with these issues. Unfortunately, these are not ideal times. Now is the time for all good men to come to the aid of their country!

Action Item 10:

Reassess Your Life's Priorities

Most of this book has dealt with economics. We have tried to make helpful suggestions as to what you might do to minimize the impact on you and your family of any potential housing price collapse. Most of our suggestions involved managing the family's finances better. We saw in Action Item 9 that it is not enough to just worry about your family's financial plan—to be truly effective it is important you become an active participant in your nation's government. Here I argue that part of the problem lies outside the traditional realm of economics theory. I will argue that there are other ways of maximizing our well-being than by maximizing the size of our home. If we can attach less importance to our physical house, we will worry less about what the future might bring as far as the potential for seeing a diminution of its market value or the potential of foreclosure and the loss of the home.

It has been said that a man's home is his castle. Ignoring the inherent gender bias, the statement can be seen as illuminating. Many of us look at our homes as the last bastion against a world we have come to distrust and in many ways dislike. We build homes that truly are fortresses, trying to keep our family free of all that we see as wrong with the world. Although lacking moats and drawbridges, our modern security systems, long driveways, and high walls and fences do an effective job of keeping the world out and our family in. It is not just the wrong kind of people we are excluding: It is the system that we wish to exclude.

We also wish to maintain an element of control and freedom in our lives. We are told what to do at work, by our government, by our friends. It is only in our homes that we maintain some sense of control. Control is a healthy component of individual liberty, but it can be debilitating if it limits our interactions and commitments to other human beings. If we become masters of our domestic universes, hiding behind our fences and brick walls, what kind of people have we become? What we gain in terms of controlling our very localized destiny we lose in terms of the fullness of our lives, devoid of human compassion and social interaction. Many American homes act as fortresses that cause families to become ever more insular. As Robert Putnam points out in his book, *Bowling Alone,* Americans are becoming less and less social over time and spending more and more time in individual pursuits.

So the American home has the potential to provide a safe and secure environment in which families can grow and prosper. But, if we are not careful, this focus on family can be all consuming to the detriment of the happiness of all the family members. Insularity is a basic reaction to insecurity, but one that worsens the condition rather than healing it. A dedicated focus solely on family does have the potential to be narcissistic as our children could be viewed as essentially DNA replicas of ourselves. Too much focus on our own well-being, and by extension on our family, can often lead to rather lonely and unfulfilled lives. Humans are at their greatest when they create social binds and exchange knowledge and culture with people completely unrelated to them.

For some, the physical home has become a large part of our life plans. A visit to a Home Depot on any Sunday morning will confirm that many Americans worship at a new altar, the holy shrine of home ownership. A 10 percent tithe would look inexpensive if we compare it to what the typical American spends each year on his home and furnishings. Again, it is wonderful that people can take such pride in their homes. It is another thing indeed when maintaining the home becomes an all-consuming part of your life. Keeping up with the Joneses can be a full-time job for many. I have a friend in New York who I used to see once every six months or so. Over a two-hour lunch I would hear about his pool, his gated security, his bathroom tile problems, and his home theater, but much less about his wife or his children or anything truly important in life. Without exception, the conversation rarely turned to my swimming pool or my leaky faucets.

So what does this have to do with a possible housing price contraction in the future? The bottom line is that we will fear it less and act more rationally in our planning if we have a more realistic perspective on what a home is. If we are discussing the unlikely probability that we might lose our homes, it is important we understand what they are, and what they are not.

First of all a home is physical structure. It is not a family. The family exists completely independent of the physical building. Please dispel any fears that if you should lose your home that your family will be in any danger. People, like cats, have a way of landing on their feet. Adversity has a way of drawing people together. Parents must avoid any associated guilt if there is a foreclosure. The belief that all will work out in the long run is usually right. We need to do a better job of separating our family's actual well-being from our home's attractiveness and comfort.

Anybody who has been poor sometime in his or her life knows two things: It is better to be rich, but you learn a tremendous amount about what is truly important in life if you don't have as many material goods getting in the way. The material goods, with which we fill our homes, seem irreplaceable, but one finds that they are not only replaceable, much of the time there is no reason to replace them. People risk their lives to go back into burning homes to save their children, their pets, and their photo albums. In the history of the world, no one has ever gone into a burning house to save a sofa, television, or washing machine.

So, to the extent that homes and their contents have become the illogical extension of mass consumerism, maybe it is time to reign in our merchandising desires. Again, violent consumerism is a hindrance, not a help, to developing warm personal relationships. Besides the time commitment of shopping and the frustration when things break or don't work, a life dedicated to one's stuff is another indication that we are spending way too much time and effort on ourselves. If we are always looking in, we will never have time to look outward, where all human warmth and kindness begins.

Michael Moore, in his wonderful documentary, *Bowling for Columbine,* argues that gun ownership is high in this country relative to other developed countries because we live in constant fear of our neighbors. Large homes provide the insularity and lack of communication necessary to breed prejudice, fear, and resentment toward our neighbors. If we lost our big house and had to move into a noisy apartment where we were forced to meet and greet our neighbors each day, it is not clear to me that we would be any worse off. I often wonder if American suburban life is not a terribly failed experiment driven by man's basic insecurities. Like most other activities, if we can overcome our own limiting insecurities we often find ourselves in a much better and more promising position. Just because we choose homes the size of castles to address our insecurities does not mean that there is not a different neighborhood-organizing principle that would provide more comfort and benefit to all.

In conclusion, part of the reason that you were attracted to this book is that you value your home so highly. You should value it as an important investment that is critical to your family's well-being. But you should also realize that there is a big and wonderful world outside of your home. Your fears of housing crashes will diminish as you place less emphasis on your home and more on your other life priorities. Your family is important, but is separate from your home. Your albums are full of photos of babies and uncles and children and proud mothers and fathers, but hopefully you have fewer candid shots of your bathrooms, kitchens, and closets.

And, I believe, if you and your family are going to be truly happy in having lived a rich and rewarding life, it is essential that they and you develop friendships and relationships outside the home. If home ownership has become too all-consuming for you, then maybe it is time you really consider downsizing your home investment. Our lives have meaning only in so much as we interact productively, emotionally, and spiritually with our community. Let us hope that, regardless of what happens to home prices in the future, we never lose sight of this important truth.

Index

f = figure; t = table

About the Author

John Talbott is currently working full time on economic research, various academic papers, and a number of political and economic texts. He is a Visiting Scholar to the Anderson School at UCLA. His major area of focus has been on examining what the root causes of a country's prosperity might be and searching for solutions to world economic and political problems.

John began his professional career working as an engineer for Bechtel Corporation. He received his MBA in finance from UCLA and worked for nine years on Wall Street as an investment banker for Goldman Sachs. He was a founding member of Goldman's LBO group, served on the firm's new product committee, and was the only nonpartner to serve on the firm's strategic planning committee.